"*Holy Goals for Body and Soul* is the perfect reminder that the lessons of sports apply to every aspect of life."

Bobby Hull
Chicago Blackhawks
Hall of Fame Left Winger

"Who better than a Catholic bishop who plays goalie to make the connections between the challenges and rewards of sports with those of daily living? *Holy Goals for Body and Soul* is a must-read for anyone seeking to be a better person."

Tony Esposito
Chicago Blackhawks
Hall of Fame Goalie

"At the risk of mixing sports metaphors, Bishop Paprocki has hit a home run with *Holy Goals for the Body and Soul.* He insightfully and inspirationally explains why God should be central to all aspects of our life, including sports. His faith-filled witness and stories from the ice and marathon course provide a modern day application of St. Paul's many scriptural exhortations to apply the lessons of sports to the spiritual life. This work is a valuable contribution to the emerging and evolving dialogue regarding the intersection of sports and faith. Specifically, it reminds us that sports, properly understood, require the interaction of the body, mind, *and* soul."

Ray McKenna
President
Catholic Athletes for Christ

"In our sports-crazy society, we sometimes overlook the good that can come from being in athletics. In *Holy Goals for Body and Soul*, Bishop Thomas Paprocki examines the characteristics that are important to all of us that play, coach, or are fans of sports. He gives us eight steps for overcoming obstacles that we face regularly in our athletic lives and connects them to God and faith. These guidelines are not only a positive approach to sports, but also to how we can use them in our daily lives."

Jeff Jackson
Head Hockey Coach
University of Notre Dame

"*Holy Goals for Body and Soul* by Bishop Paprocki is a remarkable story centered on his lifetime walk through sports and his correlation of sports and spirituality. As a young boy, Bishop Paprocki played ice hockey, and even today—as Bishop of Springfield—has stepped into the nets as goalie, notably with the Chicago Blackhawks. In this remarkable book, he outlines eight steps from his own encounters on and off the ice that can help us be better athletes, better family members, better Catholics—better 'team players.' *Holy Goals for Body and Soul* engages the reader; challenges the reader to push the envelope, to seek the higher, better goal; and like any sport we are passionate about, beckons us to enter in and partake, to strap on our skates or running shoes and go for it! A must for every athlete and every athletic administrator's bookshelf, Bishop Paprocki's book brings us with him into the struggle 'inside the net' where we can examine our own athletic experiences and encounter, through his wisdom and guidance, holiness."

Susan Saint Sing
Author of *Spirituality of Sport*

"*Holy Goals for Body and Soul* is a refreshing reminder that sports can have a powerful impact on each and every one of us who participate. The author captures the important ingredient that helps us overcome failure while developing lifelong friendships. In addition, *Holy Goals for Body and Soul* highlights the lessons of working with others to achieve and fail together. A must-read for every parent searching for the positive, long-lasting impact that sports can have."

Jay Blunk
Executive Vice President of Business Operations
Chicago Blackhawks

"I am often asked what my best call was from the over 2,000 NHL games that I worked as a referee. My best call was clearly not one I made on the ice but the ongoing call that I finally responded to from the Holy Spirit; a call that led to a lively conversion of my heart and the richness of being received into his holy Catholic Church. God, in his infinite mercy and love, continues to call each one of us home to him in various ways. He places his shepherds on earth in our path to herd lost sheep like me and tend to his flock. God chose Bishop Tom Paprocki not just to stop pucks as the 'Holy Goalie,' but most importantly as one of his special shepherds to save souls. As you hold this treasure in your hands I urge you to ask yourself if God is calling you at this very moment through these pages. Don't hesitate, because, like me, I assure you it will be the best call you can ever make!"

Kerry Fraser
Retired National Hockey League Referee

"*Holy Goals for Body and Soul* offers practical strategies for building a bridge between sports and faith. Sometimes sports teach the wrong lessons. When sports are done with an intentional connection to faith, our young people can discover and develop Christian virtues that thrive on the field and in their daily lives. Winning becomes living as a faithful disciple of Jesus. Thanks to Bishop Tom and his brother Joe for helping us keep our eye on the Gospel prize through sports. I do wonder: who won when they played against each other?"

Greg Dobie Moser
Former Executive Director, National CYO Sports
Member of the US Olympic Committee

"A bishop who runs marathons and plays hockey?! Our Catholic faith is so cool! Just as Jesus taught about the kingdom and the way to peace using familiar metaphors, Bishop Paprocki draws on our love of sports to teach essential truths of the faith. *Holy Goals for Body and Soul* integrates relatable physical objectives with practical spiritual progression, training readers to set their sights on the Lord. The only thing I loved more than his use of many sports themes is how exuberant and approachable he makes the office of bishop."

Cindy Black
Director of Youth, Young Adult, and Campus Ministry
Diocese of Fort Wayne-South Bend

HOLY GOALS FOR BODY AND SOUL

EIGHT STEPS TO CONNECT SPORTS WITH GOD AND FAITH

BISHOP THOMAS JOHN PAPROCKI
WITH JOE PAPROCKI

ave maria press AmP notre dame, indiana

Founded in 1865, Ave Maria Press is a ministry of the United States Province of Holy Cross.

www.avemariapress.com

Paperback: ISBN-10 1-59471-366-9, ISBN-13 978-1-59471-366-8

E-book: ISBN-10 1-59471-367-7, ISBN-13 978-1-59471-367-5

Cover image © Chicago Blackhawks

Interior photos: p. vii © Charles Cherney Photography, p.3 © Sam Lucero

Cover and text design by Brian C. Conley.

Printed and bound in the United States of America.

Library of Congress Cataloging-in-Publication Data

Paprocki, Thomas J.

Holy goals for body and soul : eight steps to connect sports with God and faith / Bishop Thomas J. Paprocki, with Joe Paprocki.

p. cm.

ISBN-13: 978-1-59471-366-8 (pbk.)

ISBN-10: 1-59471-366-9 (pbk.)

1. Sports--Religious aspects--Christianity. I. Paprocki, Joe. II. Title.

GV706.42.P36 2013

201.6796--dc23

2012039830

CONTENTS

EXCEL
BROWN

INTRODUCTION

They call me the "Holy Goalie."

Why? Perhaps the fact that I'm a Roman Catholic bishop who loves to play hockey has something to do with it. I've been a bishop since 2003 and a priest since 1978. But I've been playing hockey since the early 1960s. These days, I play regularly in an amateur league called the Masters' Hockey League, and I've even played goalie for practices with the Chicago Blackhawks and the Columbus Blue Jackets of the National Hockey League.

Of course, we don't usually associate the word "holy" with the sport of hockey. Then again, that's why I've written this book. I'd like to invite you to take a whole new look at the idea of *holiness* and recognize that it's not something confined to church buildings. Yes, I encounter holiness in my role as a bishop: in prayer, in the celebration of the sacraments—especially in the Eucharist and Confirmation—and in the many encounters I have with God's people. However, I also encounter holiness on the frozen pond otherwise known as the hockey rink. I encounter holiness while training for and running in marathons (yes, I also run marathons—eighteen of them since 1995). I encounter holiness when doing a workout at the health club. Suffice to say, holiness can be encountered (and practiced) just about anywhere.

St. Ignatius of Loyola, the founder of the Jesuits, referred to this as "finding God in all things." In my own personal experience, I have been finding God—encountering holiness—not only in my ministry as a priest and bishop, but also in the world of sports. Recognizing that many folks place a high priority on sports and physical fitness, I'm taking this opportunity to invite people to consider how athletics and faith—holiness and goalieness—can work together to lead to a greater awareness of God's presence in the midst of everyday realities that include fear, failure, frustration, fortitude, faith, friendship, family, and fun. Yes, even bishops have fun!

Before we go any further, a brief word about *holiness*. The Bible teaches us that God alone is holy (1 Samuel 2:2; Revelation 15:4). This is simply a way of saying that God is God and we are not. But Scripture also says that God has called us to share his holiness (1 Thessalonians 4:7; 1 Peter 15–16). When we use the term *holiness* to describe a human being, we are saying that this person reflects God-like qualities. And just what qualities are God-like? St. Paul gives us a clue, describing what he calls the fruits of the Spirit: "love, joy, peace, patience, kindness, goodness, faithfulness, gentleness, [and] self-control" (Galatians 5:22–23).

Judeo-Christian tradition believes that all human beings are created in the image and likeness of God. This means that all human beings are capable of reflecting these qualities—of being holy. This idea has actually been around for a long time. St. Francis de Sales wrote a book, first published in 1609, called *Introduction to the Devout Life*, whose chief insight was that the holy life does not require withdrawal from the world. He wrote that "it is an error, it is even a heresy," to hold that devotion to God is incompatible with any state of life, including that of soldiers, workers, and mothers of families.

Taking his cue from the Second Vatican Council, which emphasized this theme, Blessed Pope John Paul II wrote about what's come to be known as the "universal call to holiness" and universal means everybody, even hockey players. The pope explained that this call is especially true for baptized Christians who have the "responsibility to bear witness to it in all that they do" (*Christifideles Laici*).

So, if you thought that holiness was something reserved for us priests and bishops and other "churchy" types—such as nuns and monks in monasteries and cloisters—think again. You don't have to be a bishop to be a "holy goalie." As a bishop, however, I have a unique opportunity to speak from behind the goalie's mask about how holiness can be found in something as popular and routine as sports and fitness. I have outlined eight steps that are often associated with athletics—fear, frustration, failure, fortitude, faith, family, friendship, and fun—and I explain you how these steps indeed play a part in everything we do athletically, whether participating on a team, working out on our own, or just rooting as a fan.

My hope is that, in doing so, I will assist you in recognizing how you can encounter holiness in your everyday life activities—whether or not you're a goalie. St. Paul summed it up well, saying, "Whatever you do, do everything for the glory of God" (1 Corinthians 10:31).

STEP 1: FEAR

Fear is a common reaction to many situations in life as well as in sports. How do we respond? The Bible gives us some great ways to address our fears.

ARE YOU SURE YOU WANT TO PLAY HOCKEY TONIGHT?

My head was throbbing, my nose was stuffy, my joints were aching, my throat was parched. I had one nasty cold.

And I had agreed to play ice hockey with my buddies that evening.

So did I consider *not* playing? Not a chance! I am a goalie. If a goalie doesn't show up, there is wailing and gnashing of teeth. Grown men cry. I didn't want to be the cause of such emotional distress.

I had lunch that day with a priest friend of mine. Seeing my condition, he asked, "Are you sure you want to play hockey today?" I said, "Yes," adding to myself, "With all my heart." We would be playing outdoors, and this was a rare treat that I didn't want to miss. Most of our games were in indoor arenas. Skating outdoors was like returning to the ice age: the cold wind blowing on your face, the puck coming out of the dark sky. The year before we had played outdoors in a driving blizzard—with stickhandling through the snow, my winding up for a slap shot, the puck coming at me out of nowhere in the drifts, and adrenaline rushing through my veins. For hockey players, it doesn't get any better than that.

Did I want to play? Yeah, you bet I did! I wasn't about to let a little distraction like a cold hold me back.

So I went to the rink. I suited up: pads, gloves, skates, helmet, stick. I took the ice.

I was afraid.

Not that I might be too sick to play. I was afraid that I would make a fool of myself. I was afraid that my nickname, the "Holy Goalie," might be misunderstood to mean that shooters were finding too many holes in my game. I was afraid that some of the guys would mistake my sickness for my being too old and washed up. I was afraid I might hear the ultimate taunt, "Get off the ice!"

So, as I took the ice, I said a prayer: "Lord, I've got nothing today. Please help me. I'm in your hands."

At long last, the game started. The rush came at me. The puck came across the slot and I slid across the goalie crease. As the pass connected with the streaking center, his shot came point blank, hit me in the shoulder, and bounced out of harm's way. "Thank you, Jesus. Thank you, Mary. Thank you, Joseph. Thank you, my Guardian Angel." The first save is always big. At least they wouldn't be chasing me off the ice after just one shot.

On the next rush, the left winger skated behind the net. He tried to pass to his center in the slot in front of my net. I got my stick out and blocked his pass, but in doing so I sprawled out on the ice. The puck bounced back to the center in front of me. This time he lobbed a pass over my prone body that connected with one of his teammates who bagged it into the net before I could get back up. Oh well, we were down 1–0.

The next shot at me was targeted for the "five hole," between my legs. I just barely got down in time to stop it under my leg pads. "Thank you, Jesus." On the next shot, however, I wasn't as lucky. Now, we were down 2–0.

"Uh-oh. This could be a long night. Thy will be done."

Then, unexpectedly, the tide turned. I made a glove save on one shot. On another, I slid across the crease and trapped the puck in my midsection without giving up a rebound. Then, something wonderful happened. My team scored. Not once, but again. And again. Then another. And one more time for good measure. We ended up winning the game 5–2. Just before the clock ran out, my friend Wally skated in on me on a breakaway. I dropped to my knees and blocked his shot with my pads. "Nice save, Padre," said Wally, as he skated past. I stayed on my knees. "Glory be to the Father, and to the Son, and to the Holy Spirit, as it was in the beginning, is now and ever shall be, world without end. Amen."

FEAR: THE GREAT MOTIVATOR

In athletics, sometimes fear can be a great motivator. Fear and playing goalie seem to go hand in hand. Two of my childhood heroes are Chicago Blackhawks goalies Glenn Hall and Tony Esposito, who are both members of the National Hockey League Hall of Fame. Yet both were infamous for their pregame fears. Glenn Hall holds the NHL record for consecutive games played: 502. Legend has it that he used to "toss his cookies" before most games. If he didn't, he knew his mind wasn't focused properly. Tony Esposito holds the NHL record for most shutouts in a season: fifteen. His wife says that Tony wouldn't talk to her on game days. He wasn't giving her the silent treatment; he was just mentally focused on the task at hand.

Many people would assume that what frightens goalies is standing in front of a hockey net and having frozen pucks made of hard, vulcanized rubber being shot at them at speeds of 100 miles per hour. Both Glenn Hall and Tony Esposito said that's not what scared them. Most goalies would agree, and so do I. Over the years, I've had my share of injuries: cracked cartilage in my knee requiring surgery and hospitalization for a week (in the old days before outpatient arthroscopic surgery); broken fingers on my catching hand; stitches and scars on my face from pucks hitting my mask; and more black-and-blue marks and bruises on my arms, chest, and thighs than I could ever count or remember. None of that scares me or prevents me from getting back in the nets as soon as possible.

So what scares the daylights out of a goalie?

That's simple: giving up goals. Bad goals. Soft goals. Any goals. And, not only that, but especially the embarrassment that goes along with it.

Goaltending is the only position in all of sports where your failure is brought to everyone's attention with the flashing of a red light, the referee blowing his whistle and pointing at the puck in the net behind you, your opponents raising their sticks, their fans on their feet cheering, and your own fans moaning and booing.

So why do we goalies do it?

Despite the danger of being the goat, we can't resist the opportunity to rise up to the challenge. We get to be at the center of the action. We're the last line of defense. We're everyone's last hope. We're the one everyone's relying on. And that challenge is absolutely thrilling. Fear is just one part of the bigger reality we call goaltending.

HOW DO WE FACE OUR FEARS?

After winning the gold medal in 1998 as goaltender for the US Women's Hockey team at the Olympics in Nagano, Japan, Sarah Tueting pretty much walked away from the sport. She didn't even put on skates for another nine months. The lure of chasing after the challenge, however, would not let go, and when training camp opened for the 2002 Olympics, Sarah was right back in the mix, vying for the starting position. It was then that she says she faced her greatest fear: "I was scared I wouldn't make it again."

However, Sarah changed her way of thinking. "There is a risk involved in putting my life on hold, but that is not a good reason not to play," she said. "God forbid I don't make it, but I've quit hockey before and come back pretty confident in other areas of my life, so it wouldn't be that devastating." With this new way of thinking, Sarah was able to face her fears. She went on to make the team, earning a silver medal at the 2002 Winter Olympics in Salt Lake City.

Of course, playing goalie isn't the only thing that instills fear in one's heart. Fear is a common reaction to many experiences in life. I remember being afraid on the first day of school in kindergarten, which I considered to be a strange place with people I didn't know. When my mother dropped me off, I cried and didn't stop crying until she promised me a bubble-gum cigar when I got home if I would be quiet. It worked.

As time moves on and we mature, we tend to overcome certain fears. However, many fears still remain:

- Many of us are terrified of public speaking.
- We might be anxious about meeting new people or starting a new job.
- We fear taking tests.
- We can be afraid of going to the dentist.
- We fear encountering conflict.
- We await the results of a medical exam with trepidation.
- We break out in a cold sweat and our hearts race when we have to deliver some bad news or confront a person's wrongdoing or mistake.

WAYS TO FACE OUR FEARS

So, how do we face our fears? One reaction is flight. It's human nature to avoid situations that make us afraid. However, fleeing from our fears need not be the only option. Facing up to our fears helps us to grow, strengthening emotional and spiritual muscles that we will call upon in the future.

What we need are ways to deal with common, everyday fears if we don't want to become paralyzed by them. I found some excellent advice about dealing with fear as I was preparing for one of the many marathons I've run over the years. An article in *Runner's World* magazine described the fears that runners often face and how to overcome them. I think that the logic suggested here for dealing with fears in the world of running can be applied to many situations, in sports and life in general:

Example 1

Fear: "I want to enter a race, but I'm afraid I'll be last."

Solution: Most community events attract recreational walkers, so sorry, the last-place position is already taken. Ask your runner friends or the staff at local running stores about which races are most fun for

	a beginner—meaning they attract runners of all abilities and have a supportive cheering section.
Example 2	
Fear:	"When I race, everyone seems faster than me."
Solution:	There will always be runners that are faster than you. As long as you can finish within the allotted time, run and walk however you want.
Example 3	
Fear:	"I'm worried I'll hurt myself if I go faster."
Solution:	If you gradually increase your speed and distance, and incorporate sufficient walk breaks and rest days, there's little chance you'll suffer an injury.

Fears like these race as sort of a narrative through our minds. However, if we stop to think about them rationally, we can find ways of overcoming these fears. The fact is, many of our fears are based on faulty thinking. The solution, obviously, is to use our God-given brains to replace faulty thinking (referred to as "stinking thinking" in 12 Step programs) with healthy thinking. When Jesus preached the kingdom of God, it was really a call to conversion. And conversion is nothing other than a change of mind and heart—a new way of thinking. Faith and hope enable us to consider new possibilities and a new reality—a reality that is transformed.

I remember as a boy learning that three of my grandparents died in their fifties before I was born. I knew enough to realize that this was not a good gene pool. I began to fear that the same fate awaited me. This feeling of fear could have consumed me. I could have remained in fear all of my life, dreading the day when my heart would give out just as my grandparents' hearts did.

Instead, I changed my thinking. I read some articles and books about the emerging science of aerobic training and the cardiovascular benefits of rigorous endurance exercise like running. Armed with this new thinking, I started running. It was as simple as that. I had never run track or cross country in high school. My new way of thinking, grounded in hope and faith, was in essence a way of reshuffling the deck and playing with a new hand other than the one dealt to me at birth. I chose not to live in fear but instead embraced God's invitation to trust. With God's grace, today my weight is the same now as it was when I graduated high school, my blood pressure is low, my heart rate is efficient, my cholesterol is great, and I've outlived those three grandparents!

LETTING GO OF ALL THAT WE FEAR TO LOSE

Fear also plays a prominent role in many great Hollywood movies. One of my favorites is the *Star Wars* epic, which I once had the opportunity to watch in its entirety and in chronological sequence while on vacation. What becomes apparent in watching them in order from episodes one to six is how the clear thread of fear connects with the issues of redemption and trust from start to finish.

Anakin Skywalker, who appears in *Star Wars I* as a young boy with the promise of becoming the "chosen one" whom the Jedi Knights awaited, is ultimately unable to trust the power of "the Force" and instead goes over to the "Dark Side" to become the notorious Darth Vader in service of the evil empire. His own fears render him incapable of trusting and compel him to instill fear in others through his malicious cruelty. Despite his wretched and evil perversity, his son, Luke Skywalker, never gives up on his father. In *Star Wars VI*, Luke says repeatedly about his father, "I see some good in him." Luke's faith in his father is ultimately vindicated when Anakin Skywalker renounces his Darth Vader persona and saves his son's life and his own soul by killing the evil emperor—hence, redemption.

In between the innocent beginning and the happy ending of this saga is the ongoing struggle between good and evil—trust and fear—characterized by the

Jedi Knights who confront evil by use of the Force. Many of the wisest lessons in regard to working with the Force are taught by the elderly and diminutive Jedi Master, Yoda. At the beginning of Anakin Skywalker's training as a Jedi Knight, Yoda says to him at the Jedi Council, "Fear is the path to the Dark Side. Fear leads to anger, anger leads to hate; hate leads to suffering. I sense much fear in you."

Before Anakin Skywalker goes over the Dark Side, Yoda tells him, "Attachment leads to jealousy. The shadow of greed that is. Train yourself to let go of all that you fear to lose."

Yoda is describing what many great Catholic mystics would call "detachment." Through detachment, we learn to let go of all that we fear to lose, whether that is power, riches, glory, winning, success, good health, or even life on earth. In place of all these, we are called to put our hope and our trust in God. Fear is indeed the path to darkness—the inability to see clearly. Jesus, the Light of the World, dispels all darkness and thus removes the fear that can lead us to anger, hate, and suffering. Christian rock singer Stephen Curtis Chapman accurately expresses the attitude that Christians rely on when faced with fear in his composition *Hold on to Jesus*:

I have come to this ocean,
And the waves of fear are starting to grow.
The doubts and questions are rising with the
tide,
So I'm clinging to the one sure thing I know.

I will hold on to the hand of my Savior.
And I will hold on with all my might.
I will hold loosely to things that are fleeting.
And hold on to Jesus . . . I will hold on to
Jesus for life.

BE NOT AFRAID

When I was a very young priest—in 1978, to be exact—Cardinal Karol Wojtyła was elected pope. It was an electric moment when the newly elected Pope John Paul II came to the balcony to greet the throngs that had gathered in St. Peter's Square to catch a glimpse of their new Holy Father. The words he spoke to the crowds and to the world are etched in my memory: "Be not afraid." I have often thought that he was giving himself a pep talk rather than trying to reassure his listeners. After all, what did we have to be afraid of? Was the fact that he was the first non-Italian pope in over four hundred years supposed to make us nervous? I don't think so. Maybe he thought his Polish nationality would make people anxious. Being of Polish ancestry myself, I certainly wasn't frightened by his heritage!

On the other hand, the prospect of being the successor of St. Peter and the Vicar of Christ leading over a billion Catholics on earth would certainly scare me a lot more than putting on the goalie pads and facing some slap shots! Yes, someday in the future Pope John Paul II will most likely be canonized a saint, yet he would not have been human if his election as Supreme Pontiff didn't arouse some fear and trepidation in his soul.

So, it was natural for him to say, "Be not afraid." And these were much more than his own words of reassurance. In fact, he was quoting scripture. The Bible is replete with stories of people responding to God's call with fear only to be reassured with the words "be not afraid" or some slight variation thereof. Here are just a few examples:

- In the Book of Deuteronomy, God reassures Moses and the people of Israel: "It is the Lord who marches before you; he will be with you and will never forsake you. So do not fear or be dismayed" (Deuteronomy 31:8).
- In the Book of Isaiah, the LORD says, "Fear not, I am with you; be not dismayed, I am your God. I will strengthen you, and help you, and uphold you with my right hand of justice" (Isaiah 41:10, 13).

- In the Book of Proverbs we read, “Be not afraid of sudden terror, of the ruin of the wicked when it comes; for the Lord will be your confidence, and will keep your foot from being caught” (Proverbs 3:25–26).
- In the New Testament, when the angel Gabriel appears to Mary and greets her, “she was greatly troubled at what was said and pondered what sort of greeting this might be. Then the angel said to her, ‘Do not be afraid, Mary, for you have found favor with God’” (Luke 1:29–30).
- When a violent and surprise storm on the lake made the disciples fear they were going to die, they awakened Jesus who calmed the storm, saying, “Quiet, be still!” Then he asked his disciples, “Why are you terrified? Do you not yet have faith?” (Mark 4:35–40).
- In the Second Letter to Timothy, St. Paul points out that “God did not give us a spirit of cowardice but rather of power and self-control” (2 Timothy 1:7).

These are just some of the many ways that the Word of God assures us that we have nothing to fear if we place our hope and our trust in the Lord—whether we have just been elected pope or are simply facing some flying pucks.

FACING OUR GREATEST FEAR: DEATH

Perhaps the greatest fear that we all have to face is death. For those who do not believe in an afterlife, death is absolute oblivion. Ironically, belief in eternal life can also be frightening. In his 2007 encyclical letter on hope, *Spe Salvi*, Pope Benedict XVI addresses this fear:

> Faith is the substance of hope. But then the question arises: do we really want this—to live eternally? Perhaps many people reject the faith today simply because they do not find the prospect of eternal life attractive. What they desire is not eternal life at all, but this present life, for which faith in eternal life seems something of an impediment. To continue living forever—endlessly—appears more like a curse than a gift. Death, admittedly, one would wish to postpone for as long as possible. But to live always, without end—this, all things considered, can only be monotonous and ultimately unbearable.

The pope then quotes St. Ambrose, one of the Church Fathers, in the funeral discourse for his deceased brother Satyrus:

> Death was not part of nature; it became part of nature. God did not decree death from the beginning; he prescribed it as a remedy. Human life, because of sin . . . began to experience the burden of wretchedness in

> unremitting labor and unbearable sorrow. There had to be a limit to its evils; death had to restore what life had forfeited. Without the assistance of grace, immortality is more of a burden than a blessing.

One of the seeds planted in my mind as a young boy that grew into my vocation as a priest and now as a bishop was first hearing about concepts like infinity and eternal life. My young mind could not wrap itself around the possibility of something having no beginning or end. I would lie awake at night feeling frightened thinking about these mysteries. Frankly, I still do at times. That's why we call them mysteries. But I found solace as a young boy watching my parents, feeling their love and observing their faith, hope, and trust, even in the face of many great challenges, and knowing that everything would be all right. Their fear of the Lord was not trepidation or trembling before an angry God; it was a fear of doing anything that would displease such a loving and merciful God. This was a God that they eagerly sought to know better in this life and with whom they longed to spend an eternity.

Today, I recognize our Blessed Mother and Christ our Savior leading us to our Father in heaven through the Holy Spirit. I feel their love, I trust in their presence, and I confidently hope in a future—indeed, in an eternity—in which everything will be all right. Pope Benedict XVI puts it this way:

> Obviously there is a contradiction in our attitude, which points to an inner contradiction in our very existence. On the one hand, we do not want to die; above all, those who love us do not want us to die. Yet on the other hand, neither do we want to continue living indefinitely, nor was the earth created with that in view. So what do we really want? Our paradoxical attitude gives rise to a deeper question: what in fact is "life"? And what does "eternity" really mean? There are moments when it suddenly seems clear to us: yes, this is what true "life" is—this is what it should be like. Besides, what we call "life" in our everyday language is not real "life" at all. St. Augustine, in the extended letter on prayer which he addressed to Proba, a wealthy Roman widow and mother of three consuls, once wrote this: ultimately we want only one thing—"the blessed life," the life which is simply life, simply "happiness." In the final analysis, there is nothing else that we ask for in prayer. Our journey has no other goal—it is about this alone.

In the end, indeed we have nothing to fear, because if God can overcome death, as he did in raising Jesus from the dead, he can overcome anything. And so, our everyday fears need not get the best of us. We just need to change our way of thinking and put on the mind of Christ, from whose love we can never be separated.

QUOTATION

Fear is a greater evil than evil itself.

—St. Francis de Sales

PROMISE

One way I will use fear as a motivator to achieve is to . . .

PRAYER

O God, you spoke through angels and prophets, "Fear not, for I am with you." Help us to have trust in your promise to be with us always, that your abiding presence in our midst may dispel all of our fears. We ask this through Christ our Lord. Amen.

STEP 2: FRUSTRATION

Learning a sport can be difficult, and succeeding in it can be challenging. Despite such frustrations, we can succeed if we don't give up.

Growing up in Chicago in the middle to later part of the twentieth century meant one thing when it came to sports: *Frustration!* Consider the fact that the first Chicago championship I was old enough to truly enjoy (I was thirty-three at the time) occurred in 1985 when the Chicago Bears won the Super Bowl. Until that year, we Chicagoans had been waiting:

- Twenty-two years since the last Bears' championship
- Twenty-four years since the last Chicago Blackhawks Stanley Cup championship (a wait that extended to forty-nine years, ending in 2010!)

- Sixty-eight years since the last Chicago White Sox World Series championship (a wait that extended to 88 years, ending in 2005!)
- Seventy-seven years since the last Chicago Cubs World Series championship (as of the writing of this book, that drought was now at 104 years!)

Moreover, at that time, the Chicago Bulls had not won an NBA championship in franchise history since the team was established in 1966. That wait lasted twenty-five years until Michael Jordan came along to end the frustration in 1990–91.

As a hockey fan, perhaps the greatest frustration I recall took place in the 1971 Stanley Cup finals. The Blackhawks, led by high-flying Bobby Hull and Stan Mikita and anchored by goalie Tony Esposito, were the favorites to win it all. Unfortunately, the Montreal Canadiens had a different idea. The Stanley Cup finals came down to a dramatic game seven at the old Chicago Stadium, and the anticipation of the first Stanley Cup victory in Chicago in ten years filled the air. The Blackhawks jumped off to a quick 2–0 lead, and things were looking good halfway through the game. The Hawks were only thirty minutes away from winning it all. Then the unthinkable happened.

Halfway through the second period, just after Bobby Hull hit the crossbar with a shot that would have made it 3–0, Canadiens forward Jacques Lemaire took a shot from beyond the blue line, which Tony Esposito misjudged, and suddenly the Canadiens had cut the lead in half. Before long, they found a way to tie the game. Nervousness grew in Chicago as the third period proceeded. Then, veteran Canadiens forward Henri Richard came in against young Chicago defenseman Keith Magnuson, who promptly lost his balance, allowing Richard to waltz in alone and score. The Canadiens handed the Hawks a frustrating defeat on their home ice and opened a wound that would not be healed for another thirty-nine years! It was a bitter pill for me and many Chicagoans to swallow watching Montreal captain Jean Beliveau skate around the Chicago Stadium hoisting the Stanley Cup.

FRUSTRATIONS ARE PART OF SPORTS (AND LIFE ITSELF)

The fact is, frustrations are part of all sports and, yes, life itself. Even franchises known for winning (the Yankees come to mind) have experienced frustrations. Maybe not their fair share, but frustrations nonetheless! Ultimate victory is achieved by only one team or one competitor, while all others lie awake at night dreaming of what could have been. And yet, athletes forge ahead, licking their wounds, and dedicating themselves to doing better the next time around.

Not all frustrations in sports are caused by losing. Injuries often hobble athletes, causing them untold frustration as they are relegated to watching from the sidelines or the press box as their teammates continue on. One of the greatest hockey players of all time, Boston Bruins defenseman Bobby Orr, was frustrated by recurring knee problems throughout his career, resulting in six major surgeries and leading to his premature retirement at the age of thirty.

I had my own knee problems resulting from a hockey injury, nowhere near as bad as Bobby Orr's, but painful nevertheless. My injury occurred when I was in college playing in an intramural floor-hockey game. I was playing goalie, as usual, and the other team passed the puck from the right wing to the left wing at the points in my zone. The left winger took a quick shot at me as soon as he got the puck, so I was moving from my left to my right and going down to my knees to make the save, all in one move. At least I attempted to do it all in one move. Unfortunately, my knee did not get the message. I ended up twisting my right knee under my leg. I felt something pop. It didn't hurt too much, but I knew something was wrong.

What was wrong was that I couldn't straighten my leg out. I tried ice and heat for a couple of days, and nothing helped to loosen the knee joint. So I went to an orthopedic surgeon, who took x-rays and told me that a piece of my medial meniscus cartilage had chipped off and lodged in between the bones in my knee. He said I had a choice: I could have knee surgery to remove the chip, or I could walk that way with my knee bent for the rest of my life!

Don't you just love doctors with a sense of humor?

Obviously, I chose surgery, but remember: this was back in the old days before medical science developed arthroscopic surgery, which today would be done on an outpatient basis. Back then, in 1973, I had to go "under the knife," spend an entire week in the hospital, rely on crutches for two weeks, and then walk like an old man with a cane for a couple of weeks.

Talk about frustrating! Not only could I not play hockey, my day-to-day life was impacted as well. I couldn't even walk. I was amazed how quickly an unused muscle atrophies. The quad muscle in my right leg went flat. The day after the surgery, the doctor came in my room where I was lying immobile, flat on my back. He picked up my right leg by the toes six inches off the bed and said, "You'd better hold it there, 'cause I'm letting go." *Ouch*! I never felt such pain in my life, but I held my leg up mainly because I feared even worse pain if I let my leg crash back down on the bed. More pain and frustration ensued as the doctors and nurses had me out of bed the next day and I began weeks of painful and frustrating physical-rehabilitation exercises. But it all paid off: I was playing hockey again six weeks later.

I've had lots of injuries from hockey and from running that would probably scare most people away from playing goalie or running marathons. But my love for these sports always outweighed my frustration over these injuries.

USING FRUSTRATIONS FOR MOTIVATION

If you want to hear about frustration, talk to any serious athlete who is out of action because of an injury. By the same token, however, frustration can serve as a source of motivation for people with a desire to overcome the obstacle. Rehabilitation is frustrating, but it can motivate a person to work harder.

A great example of this ability to overcome frustration is pitcher Tommy John, one of my favorite baseball players of all time (and not just because we share the same names!). His 288 career victories rank him seventh of all time among left-handed pitchers in baseball history. I personally remember Tommy John from his days of pitching for the Chicago White Sox from 1965 to 1971. But his lasting claim to fame came from an incident that happened when he was pitching with the Los Angeles Dodgers in 1974. He was having a great season with a 13–3 record when he severely damaged the ulnar collateral ligament in his pitching arm. Advancements in medicine, however, provided Tommy John with the opportunity to undergo surgery using a revolutionary procedure that replaced the ligament in the elbow of his pitching arm with a tendon from his right forearm.

This surgery has come to be known as "Tommy John surgery." Tommy spent the entire 1975 season in rehab, and nobody expected him to return to baseball. One can only imagine how frustrating that must have been for him. But he didn't give up. His hard work and determination paid off as he returned the following season and pitched for fourteen more years, until he retired from the New York Yankees in 1989. Today, many pitchers have Tommy John surgery and are able to return to the game, thanks in large part to Tommy John's example that proved it could be done.

SO MANY FRUSTRATIONS!

Learning many of the skills involved in competitive sports can be frustrating in and of itself. In particular, when it comes to playing ice hockey, one has to first master the skill of gliding across a frozen sheet of ice while balanced on a thin steel blade! Learning to ice-skate is itself a frustrating endeavor, involving much falling down and getting back up again. Elbows, knees, rear ends, and egos end up bruised and battered. My own experience of learning how to skate was filled with moments of frustration.

Growing up on the south side of Chicago, there were no ice rinks near our house. That's why I started out playing floor hockey and roller hockey. It wasn't until I was in my first year at Mundelein Seminary that I started to ice-skate on the large lake at the center of the seminary campus. The weather conditions for ice-skating were perfect that particular January, with temperatures well below freezing all month and no snow. Every day that month I took my skates and got out on the ice. I remember the frustration of falling down and picking myself up repeatedly, but I also remember the joy when I was eventually able to skate all the way across the lake and back on a beautiful moonlit night.

It would still be many more years before I would play ice hockey. I was frustrated that my skating was not good enough for me to play—I needed a lot more practice skating. So, when I was working at the Archdiocese of Chicago Pastoral Center downtown, I often used my lunch break on Fridays during the winter months to head out to the public, outdoor ice rink called "Skate on State Street" with my friends Carl Klimowicz and Steve Fister. I mostly just skated in circles, but the repetition helped me to grow comfortable on the ice.

The practice paid off when one day I got a call from Steve Demitro, who runs an over-thirty, no-check hockey program called the Masters Hockey League. He said he needed a goalie and invited me to play in the league.

I explained that I had been playing goalie since childhood and had been working on my ice-skating for the past few years, but I had never put the two together. He suggested that I start out playing pick-up games called "rat hockey," which I did, and within a short time he put me on the Lawyers Hockey Team in the Masters Hockey League, made up of, well, lawyers!

I was pretty bad at first. It was really frustrating as I improved my footwork of skating forward and backward in my goalie's crease, moving laterally with the movement of the puck, and picking myself up when I would fall down. But I didn't give up, and within a couple of years we won the Masters Hockey League playoffs. In fact, in my first eleven years of playing in that league, we won the championship seven times! I don't think it was so much my perseverance as it was the patience of my teammates, especially my captain, Steve Demitro, that paid off in the end.

The skill of ice-skating—much like the skill of swimming, riding a bike, rollerblading, or skateboarding—is counterintuitive. By nature, we yearn to plant our feet on solid ground. Even something as basic as running can be frustrating. The first time I ran a mile when I was in high school at Quigley South was a horrible experience: gasping for air, feeling the burning sensation in my lungs, and *not* feeling my legs—that didn't want to move. My whole body seemed to be screaming at me: *Don't ever do that again*!

DEVELOPING NEW SKILLS TO WARD OFF FRUSTRATIONS

In order to master ice-skating or running or any of the other abilities mentioned above, we have to develop a new set of skills and even a new belief system that embraces the possibility of doing something that does not come naturally. We have to override our natural instincts and imagine the possibilities of a new way of transporting ourselves. The process is laden with frustration. Just watch an episode of *Dancing with the Stars*. Notice that as the celebrities struggle to learn dance steps, they instead end up tripping, stepping on their partner's toes, or even falling down. The frustration often results in the contestant considering the option of giving up:

- "I'm too old."
- "I'm too fat."
- "I'm too slow."
- "I'm too uncoordinated."
- "I can't remember the sequence of steps."

It takes great imagination to first visualize accomplishing new skills and then no small doses of persistence, determination, and perseverance to overcome the frustrations and ultimately succeed.

CHRISTIAN LIVING IS ALSO COUNTERINTUITIVE

The same can be said of learning how to live as a disciple of Jesus. Following the Gospel of Jesus Christ is also counterintuitive. What Jesus teaches—namely selfless love—goes against our human tendency to put ourselves first. Jesus' instructions to love our enemies, pray for our persecutors, turn the other cheek, and wash one another's feet are all counterintuitive. It is no surprise then that Jesus' disciples were often frustrated by his teachings. For example:

- When little children approached Jesus, the disciples wanted to shoo them away. They were frustrated to find out that Jesus wanted the little children to come to him.
- When Jesus spoke of his impending suffering and crucifixion, Peter objected in frustration, telling Jesus they would never let this happen to him.
- When Jesus spoke of himself as the Bread of Life, many of his followers left him because they found his teaching too difficult. They were frustrated with him.
- When Judas, one of the Apostles, was frustrated by Jesus' lack of action against Rome, he betrayed him in hopes of forcing Jesus to show his power.

The list goes on. To follow Jesus is like strapping on a pair of skates for the first time and trying to balance on a thin blade of steel as you attempt to glide across a frozen sheet of ice. To follow Jesus, one needs to undergo conversion—a change of heart and mind. It requires a new way of thinking.

FRUSTRATIONS OF THE FAITH, BIG AND SMALL

Recently a penitent expressed to me how frustrated he felt by his sins. I can't say what those sins were, but I don't recall anyone ever describing his sinfulness as frustrating. We often feel guilty, ashamed, embarrassed, penitent, and remorseful about our sins—but frustrated? The more I thought about it, though, this person's reaction should be a natural one. We should all feel frustrated when we fail in our efforts to overcome our sinfulness, live up to our ideals, and be reconciled with God and neighbor.

The process of conversion is inherently frustrating. Just look at the story of the conversion of St. Paul in chapter 9 of the Acts of the Apostles. Called Saul, he was perfectly comfortable in his role as a protector of the Jewish faith until his encounter with the Risen Christ on the road to Damascus. He was thrown to the ground, blinded, unsure of who was speaking to him, and lost for what to do next.

Saul's blindness persisted for three days, accompanied by a fever. This was not a happy man. You could call him frustrated. The first step of conversion is letting go of something we *don't* want to let go of. It is similar to watching a skater who falls to the ice and just sits there, not really wanting to get up and try again. At first, Saul didn't really want to let go of his old way of living. It was only over time—and with the help of others—that Saul came to embrace a new way of thinking that placed Jesus at the center of his life. As a result, a new person—Paul—was born.

While the story of St. Paul's conversion comes to us in condensed form over just a couple of chapters in the Acts of the Apostles, Scripture actually tells us that the process of Paul's conversion stretched over many years. The time between his encounter with the Risen Christ on the road to Damascus and the beginning of his ministry to the Gentiles was about seven years. Certainly there were more frustrations for Paul during that seven-year period. But St. Paul persevered because he had received a taste of what awaited him if he did so: fullness of life in Jesus Christ.

St. Paul also had to deal with the frustration of trying to convince skeptical listeners that Jesus was the Messiah and had risen from the dead. One example occurs in Acts 17. In Athens, Paul "grew exasperated at the sight of the city full of idols. So he debated in the synagogue with the Jews and with the worshipers, and daily in the public square with whoever happened to be there" (Acts 17:16–17).

He also engaged in debate with philosophers and other people of Athens in a place called the Areopagus. The account of his experience tells us that, "when they heard about the resurrection of the dead, some began to scoff, but others said, 'We should like to hear you on this some other time.' And so Paul left them" (Acts 17:32–33). It's not too hard to visualize the Athenians sniffing haughtily and sneering down their noses at Paul as they dismissed him. We can also sense Paul's frustration as he walked away, seemingly rejected. All was not lost, however, since we are also told that "some did join him, and became believers" (Acts 17:33).

We can learn a lot from St. Paul about how to deal with the challenge of living in today's culture. Trying to be religious in a secular society can be very frustrating. Read almost any article about religion or faith online, and you will invariably find below the article no shortage of negative and nasty comments from readers about faith, religion, and the Catholic Church. St. Paul's writings in the New Testament encourage us in these hard times:

> We are afflicted in every way, but not constrained; perplexed, but not driven to

> despair; persecuted, but not abandoned; struck down, but not destroyed; always carrying about in the body the dying of Jesus, so that the life of Jesus may also be manifested in our body. (2 Corinthians 4:8–10)

A well-known professional athlete who is famous for expressing his faith publicly is quarterback Tim Tebow. He developed an iconic celebration of victory in which he points skyward and takes a knee in prayer. He usually opens the postgame interview saying, "First, I'd like to thank my Lord and Savior, Jesus Christ." Then he closes with, "God bless." This infuriates some people and is one of the main reasons why he has gotten so much media attention. Nonbelievers don't like to hear about Jesus. Secularists want to banish expressions of faith from the public square.

Personally, I say hooray for Tim Tebow. He's doing what the Blessed Virgin Mary did, magnifying the Lord. He says that football is just a game and that God doesn't care who wins or loses. I like to say that when athletes die, God is not going to ask them at the Last Judgment what their won-lost record was. But God does care about how we use the gifts and talents that he gave us. So we should care enough to give God praise and thanksgiving for these gifts.

PERSISTENCE, DETERMINATION, AND PERSEVERANCE CAN OVERCOME FRUSTRATIONS

So what are we to do in the face of frustrations? We are called to practice perseverance, which is the child of endurance, which, in turn, is the child of patience. The Scripture is filled with calls for us to practice patience, endurance, and perseverance and to never give in to despair or frustration.

Perhaps the most compelling words about patience are found in the Letter of James, which tells us to "be patient until the coming of the Lord" (5:7). For St. James, however, being patient in the midst of frustration was not simply a matter of gritting one's teeth. It was an expression of love (see also 1 Corinthians 13:4). Likewise, the biblical call to endurance is not to be equated with passive acceptance of one's situation. It is an active determination to outlast the frustration. Despite all of the frustrations that come with nine months of child-bearing, we would never refer to a pregnant woman as someone who was "enduring" but rather as someone who was "expecting." Likewise, perseverance is an act of faith because ultimately it is the acknowledgment that, although our own strength is depleted, God will provide the strength we need.

Patience, endurance, and perseverance are all made possible by hope—the firm expectation of a better future. In fact, when you get down to it, the life of faith makes no sense whatsoever without our belief in eternal life. The only reason to patiently endure and to persevere in the face of present frustrations is the promise of eternity with God. Without that broader perspective, we are simply taking moments out of context and facing the same danger that comes with taking words out of context: misinterpretation. Hope enables us to avoid misinterpreting present frustrations as permanent. This hope is exemplified numerous times in scripture:

- Patience, endurance, and perseverance can be seen in the Exodus of the Jewish people from slavery in Egypt as they experienced the frustration of wandering the desert for forty years, propelled by the hope of entering the Promised Land.
- In Luke 18:1–8, Jesus tells the parable of widow whose request is finally granted because of her persistence, teaching us that our own prayer must be buoyed by hope and characterized by perseverance.
- Hebrews 12:1–2 says that "since we are surrounded by so great a cloud of witnesses, let us rid ourselves of every burden and sin that clings to us and persevere in running the race that lies before us, while keeping our eyes fixed on Jesus, the leader and perfecter of faith." Our eyes are not to be fixed on that which frustrates us but on Jesus who is our hope.

In addition to scripture, history also provides us with great examples of untiring perseverance. One such example is Winston Churchill, the British prime minister during World War II who served until victory had been secured over Nazi Germany. In a speech delivered October 29, 1941, he said, "Never give in. Never give in. Never, never, never, never—in nothing, great or small, large or petty—never give in, except to convictions of honor and good sense. Never yield to force. Never yield to the apparently overwhelming might of the enemy."

HOPE WINS

In short, we are called to be people of hope. Hope is more than wishful thinking. Hope is a perseverance that conquers our frustrations. Hope is described as an anchor in Hebrews 6:19, as a door in Hosea 2:15, and as a helmet in 1 Thessalonians 5:8. In other words, hope keeps us grounded, opens a path for us, and protects us on our journey. Frustrations keep us frozen in the present moment. The key to melting the ice of frustration is to draw from the past and to look to the future. For Christians, this means to draw on the stories of salvation history to see how God's great deeds have enabled his people to endure and persevere. At the same time, we are to look to the future with expectation because of the promise that the resurrection of Jesus holds for each of us, namely, a share in eternal life. This hope transforms our endurance into joyful expectation.

In his 2007 Encyclical Letter on Christian hope, *Spe Salvi*, Pope Benedict XVI wrote that our "great, true hope which holds firm in spite of all disappointments can only be God—God who has loved us and who continues to love us 'to the end,' until all 'is accomplished'" (cf. John 13:1 and 19:30). Life will not be without its frustrations. With God, our true hope, however, we can persevere in faith, knowing that when we place our trust in him, we will never be disappointed.

QUOTATION

If Christ is with us, who is against us? You can fight with confidence where you are sure of victory. With Christ and for Christ victory is certain.

—St. Bernard

PROMISE

I will not let my frustrations overcome me. I will clothe myself in hope by . . .

PRAYER

O God, you know us better than we know ourselves. You know the frustrations and anxieties that affect our souls. Keep our eyes fixed, not on those things that frustrate us, but on Jesus who is our hope. Give us the patience, endurance, and perseverance we need to jump the hurdles that obstruct the path to our goals.

May your grace enable us to achieve the fulfillment of your will for us. We ask this through Christ our Lord. Amen.

STEP 3: FAILURE

There are a lot more losers than winners in sports. How do we deal with failure?

"Did you win the race?"

The question took me by surprise. Dumbfounded, I simply asked, "What?"

A priest at a conference I was attending was the person asking the question. I didn't know him very well. I had been the Bishop of Springfield in Illinois less than two years at the time, and we only saw each other at diocesan gatherings such as these. He apparently didn't know a lot about me, either, but he had heard that I had recently run a marathon, so he repeated the question, "Did you win the race?"

"No," I answered, trying to figure out how to explain to a non–marathon runner that I don't ever expect to "win" a marathon in terms of being the first runner to cross the finish line. I wanted to explain to him that I run marathons, not to win, but rather I am competing against myself, and victory comes in achieving my goal. For some runners, that goal may be just to finish the race. For others, it's getting a qualifying time for the Boston Marathon or setting a personal record. The more I talked, the more spurious and futile my explanations seemed to be.

This man couldn't get past the idea that "winning" means more than just "finishing first." It reminded me of one of the classic *Seinfeld* episodes when the characters gathered to witness the New York City Marathon and George Costanza remarked, "A couple of runners from Kenya and 25,000 losers." I guess from that point of view I have failed to win all eighteen marathons that I've run up to this point. I have never come close to that kind of winning, and I know I never will.

The definition of winning or success in the sport of baseball might be equally hard to explain to a novice. Growing up, my brothers and I played baseball whenever and wherever we could (that's if we weren't playing hockey, of course).

We played baseball in the laundry room (with a plastic Wiffle ball and plastic bats).

We played on the sidewalk in front of our house.

We played in the alley behind our house.

We played on the boulevard.

We played at the school yard.

We played baseball of all kinds: with sponge balls, plastic balls, rubber balls, kickballs, and softballs (only the sixteen-inch, Chicago-style). When we got older we finally played with regular hardballs. We imitated all of our favorite players: Tommy John, Ernie Banks, Ron Santo, Luis Aparicio, and even players from non-Chicago teams like Willie Mays, Sandy Koufax, Harmon Killebrew, and many others.

Despite our dreams and fantasies of becoming big-league ballplayers ourselves some day, my brothers and I quickly learned one of the toughest lessons about baseball: It is a game of failure.

Consider this: Ted Williams, called by many (including himself) "the greatest hitter who ever lived," is the last player to have a .400 batting average for one season. He hit .406 with the 1941 Boston Red Sox. The more typical standard for batting excellence is a .300 average. This means the best hitters get a hit only 30 percent of the time. Ted once remarked that batters who fail only seven times out of ten attempts will go down as the greatest in their sport!

Marathon running and baseball, however, are not alone when it comes to failure. As I mentioned in an earlier chapter, in hockey, the failure of a goalie to stop the puck from entering the net is brought to the attention of all by a flashing red light, a loud horn, a referee pointing at the net, and all the players on the other team raising their sticks in celebration. At the United Center in Chicago, the goalie must then endure a few minutes of more than 20,000 people singing the "doh, doh, dee, oh" of a raucous song called "Chelsea Dagger," as they stomp, clap, and cheer wildly and loudly. At the University of Notre Dame hockey games, Irish fans taunt the opposing goalie after giving up a goal by calling his name and chanting in unison, "*You let the whole team down!*"

Everybody has good days and bad days in hockey. If you're a forward or a defenseman, you can have a bad game and make a number of mistakes, but it's possible that most people (except maybe your coach) won't notice as long as your teammates cover for you and your team wins. Not so for the goalie. In professional hockey, if the goalie is having a bad night, he might be immediately pulled from the game after giving up a goal. When that happens, the pulled goalie hangs his head in a sullen retreat to the bench, but at least then he's out of the spotlight. In my men's league, there are no backup goalies, so when I'm having a bad night, I can't even pull myself from the game as much as I might just want to disappear from the ice!

Of course, after a goalie allows a few too many goals, the effort of the whole team worsens, which just creates a snowball effect leading to more bad goals. Even though there are no fans chanting in the stands as I head to the locker room when the clock mercifully runs out, there is a chorus shouting in my head, "*Tom, you let the whole team down*!" That sentiment is only confirmed by the deafening silence of my teammates. Instead of hearing, "Nice game, Bishop Tom," there's just silence. No one wants to hurt my feelings, and everyone is too respectful to say, "Gee, you really stunk out there tonight," but I know they're thinking it; so sometimes I'll break the ice (so to speak) and say it: "I just didn't have it tonight. Sorry guys."

FAILURE IS A MATTER OF PERSPECTIVE

Of course, as we progress through life, most people come to realize that winning, which focuses only on a final score or result, really "isn't everything." Try telling that to a kid who's playing the biggest game of his life or to a professional athlete who is vying for a coveted championship. Losses and poor performance do equate with failure. Indeed, failure is a part of sports. But then again, failure is a part of life too.

We may fail at a project at school or work.

We may fail in our efforts to get accepted into a particular school, get hired by a certain company, get a book or article published, or buy our dream home.

Worse yet, we may experience the loss of a job and the sense of failure that accompanies that loss.

Sometimes we fail at relationships.

We experience failure all too often in our lives. Failure is inevitable when we are faced with so many challenges. We can either allow ourselves to be defined by that failure, or we can use it as an opportunity to learn and grow.

Don't forget, too, that failure is often a matter of perspective. I wouldn't say that anyone who finishes a marathon has "failed." I wouldn't call Ted Williams a "failure" even though in his best season he failed in almost six out of ten at bats. And certainly any boy or girl, man or woman, who is courageous enough to don the goalie pads and get in the nets to face a barrage of vulcanized pucks will never be a "failure" in my book!

WE CAN LEARN FROM FAILURE

Ironically, failure can teach a life lesson. At least that's what we've always been told. Who hasn't heard: "You can learn from your mistakes"? Bob Dylan, the famous American singer-songwriter, echoed the same message when he said that "there's no success like failure." Scientific studies seem to confirm that every mistake a person makes generates reactions in the brain. People with stronger neural reactions to failure tend to focus on the error and try to learn from it.

Psychologists at Michigan State and Stanford universities distinguished between people with a "fixed mindset," who see themselves as having a certain amount of intelligence that cannot be changed, and those with a "growth mindset," who believe that they can get better at almost anything, provided they invest the necessary time and energy. The results were borne out by tests; students who were praised for their effort tended to learn from their mistakes. Students who were praised for their aptitude didn't as much. Apparently those who believed they were smart saw their intelligence as having a fixed quota, so that if they made a mistake, they felt that there was nothing they could do about it. On the other hand, those who put in a lot of effort believed that they could overcome their mistakes if they just worked at it.

Personally, I subscribe to the view that we can all learn from our failures. When I was a freshman in college, I failed the physical-fitness test in gym class because I could not do a single chin-up. I was so mortified that I determined that I would never fail a fitness test again. I practiced doing chin-ups every day. Gradually I built up my arm strength with frequent repetitions. When I was ordained a priest, I got a chin-up bar for my room and have taken it with me whenever I've moved to another assignment. I still do fifteen chin-ups (underhand grip) and ten pull-ups (overhand grip) every other day. On the alternate days I do fifty to seventy-five push-ups. Certainly that failure as a college freshman has stayed with me and has continued to motivate me to succeed!

EVEN THE BEST OF THE BEST FAIL

Michael Jordan is an all-time basketball great. He led the Chicago Bulls to six basketball championships in the 1990s. He won the NBA's Most Valuable Player award five times. In 1999, he was named the greatest North American athlete of the twentieth century by ESPN. Jordan is a Hall of Famer, truly a giant in the game. However, as a sophomore in high school, Michael Jordan's high school coach thought he was too short. (Michael was 5′11″ at the time.) The coach sent one of the greatest players ever down to the junior varsity team.

This roadblock to success wasn't the only one Michael would ever experience. He noted: "I missed more than nine thousand shots in my career. I lost almost three hundred games. On twenty-six occasions that I was entrusted to take the game winning shot, I missed. I have failed over and over and over again in my life. And that is why I succeed."

Or, think about Abraham Lincoln, the sixteenth president of the United States. Prior to his election, Abraham Lincoln was a successful lawyer who served three terms in the Illinois General Assembly and one term in the United States Congress. However, he also experienced a number of failures in his life:

- In 1832, he was defeated in his first bid for a seat in the Illinois legislature.
- In 1833, he failed in business and incurred considerable debt.
- In 1843, he was defeated in his first attempt at nomination for Congress.
- In 1849, he was rejected for the position of land officer.
- In 1854, he lost his first election for the United States Senate.
- In 1856, he was defeated for the nomination as vice president.
- In 1858, he failed again to win a seat in the United States Senate.

One might also say that, as president, Abraham Lincoln failed in his first several attempts to select capable generals to lead the Union Army in the Civil War. There were many failed battles, especially in the early stages of the war. Of course, as we know, he eventually found a successful general in Ulysses S. Grant, who led the Union to victory and came to be known as one of the greatest, if not the greatest, presidents in United States history for healing the nation from Civil War.

The only way to avoid failure entirely is simply to never even try. It would have been unthinkable for President Lincoln to have not even tried to save the Union. President Theodore Roosevelt echoed this point of view in a speech at the Sorbonne in Paris on April 23, 1910: "It is not the critic who counts: not the one who points out how the strong man stumbles or where the doer of deeds could have done better. The credit belongs to the man who is actually in the arena . . . if he fails, at least he fails while daring greatly, so that his place shall never be with those cold and timid souls who knew neither victory nor defeat."

If we need any more convincing of the value in learning from and overcoming failure, we only have to look to Jesus. The gospels record several instances when, in our limited human terms, we might think of what Jesus did as failure. For example:

- In Nazareth he was unable to do many miracles because of their lack of faith (Matthew 13:58).
- When he preached in the synagogue, he offended the people (Mark 6:3).
- On one occasion people in the synagogue were so angered by his words that they tried to push him off a cliff (Luke 4:14–30).
- He was unable to convince a rich young man to follow him (Luke 18:18).

- When he tried to heal a blind man, it took him two tries (Mark 8:22–26)

As with Michael Jordan and Abraham Lincoln, Jesus' "failures" ultimately resulted in success. Ultimate success. The Letter to the Hebrews reminds us that "we do not have a high priest who is unable to sympathize with our weaknesses, but one who has similarly been test in every way, but without sin" (4:15).

TROPHIES OF SPORT AND THE CROSS OF FAITH

In sports, success is noted and celebrated with trophies. These golden symbols of success are awarded for both individual honors and team championships. I would have to say that the greatest of all trophies is the Stanley Cup, given annually to the National Hockey League champion. Baseball, basketball, and football have their own championship trophies, but each year the winning team is awarded a replica so that the new champion can keep a copy on display at its home arena or stadium. The Stanley Cup is different. The trophy was donated in 1892 by then–Governor General of Canada, the Lord Stanley of Preston, as an award for Canada's top-ranking amateur ice-hockey club. It has been used as the NHL's trophy since 1926. The team that wins it is only allowed to keep it until a new team wins it the following year.

When the Chicago Blackhawks won the Stanley Cup in 2010, I joined my brother Joe and his wife, Joanne, and my brother Al and his son Ian and thousands of other fans who jammed the victory parade in downtown Chicago. We were mainly there to get a glimpse of the Stanley Cup. I got an even closer look at the cup when it was brought to the governor's mansion in Springfield that summer. It is an awesome trophy due to its storied history and its enormous prestige.

Which brings me to the ultimate symbol of victory: the Cross of Jesus Christ. The Cross would seem to be a symbol of failure, but in fact the Cross is our trophy of success.

Many people wear a cross around their necks.

Catholic schools have crucifixes in their classrooms.

Some people have crucifixes on the dashboard of their cars.

Bishops wear a pectoral cross as a reminder to keep Christ close to their hearts.

At Mass, we carry the crucifix in procession.

Do you think we would really display a symbol of failure? In fact, through the Cross, Christ overcame failure. When Jesus was executed by crucifixion, the people around him, both his friends and his opponents, most likely viewed that event as the culminating failure of his life. Jesus turned that apparent failure into a magnificent success. Through the Cross, Christ defeated sin and death.

The Cross is the symbol of ultimate success and victory.

WE CAN OVERCOME FAILURE AND SIN

Most failures in life are morally neutral. It is not a sin (thank goodness!) if I fail to prevent a goal or if I fail to finish a marathon, unless my failure is due to my intentionally not using the gifts and talents that God gave me. But the lessons of sinfulness, repentance, and conversion can teach us how to overcome our failures—both those that are sins and those that are not.

When we do sin, we fail to act as God expects us to act. Sin is a failure to love. Think about these examples from the Bible:

- The story of Noah and the ark tells of God's punishment for the sins of humanity, but it ends with God sending a rainbow to serve as a sign of his merciful promise never to unleash such a punishment again (Genesis 6–9).
- Abraham interceded for the sinful people of Sodom to save them from God's justifiable wrath (Genesis 18:16–33).
- Moses pleaded with God not to punish the people when they turned to idolatry and fashioned the molten calf as their false god (Exodus 32:1–14).

- Jesus frequently combined his physical healing of the infirm with the forgiveness of their sins (Matthew 9:6 and Luke 5:24).
- Jesus saved the woman caught in adultery from being stoned to death and refused to join in her condemnation, sending her on her way with the admonition to sin no more (John 7:53–8:11).
- Jesus not only forgave Peter for denying him but gave Peter and the other Apostles (and their successors) the power to forgive sins on his behalf (Matthew 16:18–19).

However, even when we sin, God does not stop loving us. When Catholics go to confession (the Sacrament of Penance), we encounter a tangible experience of God's grace overcoming our sinful failures when we hear the priest say aloud the words of absolution. Reconciliation is a powerful dynamic that restores a relationship ruptured by sin.

Sinfulness and failure of humans and the human condition are not the final word. Time and time again, God has demonstrated his power to overcome human limitation. Never forget the life and example of the Blessed Virgin Mary, who conceived her child by the power of the Holy Spirit, "for nothing is impossible for God" (Luke 1:26–38).

WE CELEBRATE GOD'S VICTORY

Chicago Blackhawks Hall of Fame goaltender Glenn Hall was on the 1961 Stanley Cup champion Blackhawks, but in the chaos of the celebration, he never got to hoist the Cup. In 2010, as the Blackhawks' more recent Stanley Cup was touring Canada, it made a stop at Glenn Hall's home. Glenn triumphantly hoisted the Cup over his head and took pride in seeing his name etched into the trophy along with his fellow 1961 Blackhawks.

The Cup's curator mentioned to Glenn that his name was inscribed elsewhere on the trophy. Glenn said that he knew that. "Yes, in 1989, I was the goalie coach for the Calgary Flames so my name is engraved with that team." The curator responded, "No, I mean as a player. You're also engraved with the 1952 Detroit Red Wings." Glenn had no idea that was true, since he didn't play a minute with the Red Wings that season. But he was associated with the Red Wings minor-league affiliate in Indianapolis. How excited he was to learn, over fifty years later, that he was already a champion simply by association! The 1952 Red Wings had generously allowed him to share in their triumph.

We, too, are invited to share in someone else's triumph. Despite *our* failures, God invites us to celebrate *his* victory. We don't need to do anything to earn this invitation. In fact, it cannot be earned. We only need to associate ourselves with Christ the Victor and remain loyal to him. The prophet Isaiah describes a victory banquet celebrating God's triumphs, saying "On this mountain the Lord Almighty will prepare a feast of rich food for all peoples, a banquet of aged wine—the best of meats and the finest of wines" (Isaiah 25:6–10).

Who wouldn't want to be invited to a banquet where the host takes away our failures and instead invites us to celebrate his victory?

QUOTATION

So you have failed? You cannot fail. You have not failed: you have gained experience. Forward!

—Venerable José Escriva

PROMISE

I will refocus my goals after learning from my failures. I will combine my own failure with the Cross of Christ by . . .

PRAYER

O God, you did not create us for failure, but to share in your glory. When we fall, may your grace lift us up. Do not let us be obsessed with winning, but help us to be victorious in your sight by using the gifts and talents that you gave us to the best of our ability. We ask this through Christ our Lord. Amen.

STEP 4: FORTITUDE

Many athletic activities require fortitude, a virtue that gives us strength to face the challenges of life.

Have you ever noticed how effortlessly elite runners seem to glide through their training? As I work through my speed workouts huffing and puffing, straining my muscles, and testing my willpower to pick up the pace, it certainly seems to me that the people on the track passing me by do so with ease. Seeing them excel seemingly without a sweat may give rise to the vice of envy, but that's a subject for another time.

In the previous steps, we addressed some negative forces that we all face in sports and in life: fear, frustrations, and failures. Fortunately, there are some positive antidotes. In step 4, we will explore the virtue of fortitude, or courage, as a way to overcome our challenges.

We would be mistaken to think that any success in life comes without deep reserves of inner fortitude. Marathoners can relate to the necessity of inner fortitude. I'm guessing that there are not many marathoners who are able to avoid "hitting the wall," a term to describe the combination of body fatigue and mental confusion that creeps up in the last stages of a marathon, usually after mile 21. In a recent *Runner's World* article, forty-one-year-old marathoner Adam Buckley Cohen recalled how he overcame "the wall" in the 2010 Chicago Marathon: "In Chinatown, at mile 22, my body began to betray me. My legs seized up like drying concrete. Each stride became a struggle. My thoughts started to shift to a familiar place: *Oh, no, here comes the bonk.*"

So what did Adam do? Where many people would give up, he took a different approach: "I forced myself to think about my training pace runs. *These* are the miles I've been training for. This is why I endured all those long runs on tired legs. I can do this. *Manage the pain.*"

Notice how Adam described his digging down deep to find an inner reserve to get him through. This is fortitude. Talent and skills are certainly factors in achieving success. But they are not the only factors. Even talented and skilled people need exceptional levels of fortitude to reach incredible levels of achievement.

While I am not an elite runner, I have completed eighteen marathons as of this writing. It has been fascinating to me how some of my friends and colleagues now take it for granted that I will succeed with each marathon that I attempt. I guess that's a natural reaction when someone has a successful "track record" of accomplishment. But I seem to recall a lot more encouragement coming my way for my first few marathons as well as congratulations upon finishing. When I would tell people I was training for a marathon, they would say, "Wow! That's amazing!" When I had finished a marathon, people would express their awe at this accomplishment. Now, when I tell people I'm planning to run another marathon, the reaction often seems to be a matter-of-fact: "That's nice. Good luck." Afterward, I hear a simple, "Good job."

Now, I don't mean this as a complaint, but simply as an observation. To an outsider, it might appear that running a marathon has become a piece of cake for me. From the inside, I know that each marathon is a tough challenge that requires tremendous effort—physically, mentally, emotionally, and spiritually—to complete. It requires inner strength—in a word, fortitude.

WHAT IS FORTITUDE? WHERE DOES IT COME FROM?

Fortitude is one of the cardinal virtues, along with prudence, justice, and temperance. The word "cardinal" comes from the Latin word, *cardo,* which means "hinge." All the other virtues—for example, patience, kindness, and humility—are connected to or hinge on these four. The *Catechism of the Catholic Church* teaches that fortitude "enables one to conquer fear, even fear of death, and to face trials and persecutions. It disposes one even to renounce and sacrifice his life in defense of a just cause" (1808).

Fortitude is not something we simply possess on our own; it comes from God who is the source of all strength. Jesus reminds his disciples, "In the world you have trouble; but be of courage, I have overcome the world" (John 16:33). As the Son of God, Jesus has the strength and courage to overcome this world's trials and tribulations, and we can take courage as well, knowing that his strength is offered to us.

Fortunately, we can draw from living examples of fortitude, including many from the world of sports.

LEARNING FROM THE COURAGE OF OTHERS

Certainly the story of Adam Buckley Cohen is inspiring. I will think of his example whenever I "hit the wall"—literally and figuratively—in the future. I have also drawn fortitude from the examples of some other marathoners—and some goalies too!

At the 1908 Olympics in London, Dorando Pietri staggered across the finish line in 2:54:56. There were fifty-five other competitors, and Dorando beat them all to the finish line. However, he took a wrong turn when he entered the stadium for the last leg of the race. The umpires redirected him and even helped him up after he fell five times in the final stretch. Although he was officially disqualified because of their help (which he didn't solicit), his amazing finish demonstrated great fortitude.

A similar scene (but this time without the unsolicited assistance) was repeated at the 1984 Olympics in Los Angeles when Gabriela Andersen of Switzerland barely dragged herself across the finish line under her own power. The *Los Angeles Times* described the closing moments of the race in this way:

> In what looked like some sort of death dance . . . Andersen appeared, leaning to the left, as if some force was pulling her off the track and onto the infield. Track stewards began following her, uncertain what to do. When she saw them approach, she staggered away, fearing they would touch her, and thereby disqualify her. . . . But millions feared that

> they might be watching a woman dying. The struggle continued. Andersen's final lap seemed to take forever. For most of it, she walked—a stiff-legged gait, veering across lanes, her head and shoulders bent forward. As she approached the finish, her pace quickened and her right arm began swinging wildly. She crossed the finish line, and collapsed into the arms of three stewards.

Gabriela officially finished thirty-seventh, but the fact that she finished at all is a testimony to her extraordinary fortitude and determination.

British runner Derek Redmond was running a much shorter track event at the 1992 Summer Olympics in Barcelona when he tore a hamstring muscle in the 400-meter semifinal heat. After getting off to a good start, he pulled up lame, clutching his right leg. He came to a full stop in a crouched position, his head in his hands, as the other runners sprinted ahead across the finish line. Then, to the surprise of all, he stood up and began hopping on his good leg around the track, making for the finish line. As the crowd stood and cheered, Derek's father ran out onto the track and helped his sobbing son across the finish line. Later, his dad explained that he knew his son had to finish no matter what happened and that he was there to help him across the line. Sometimes we can draw courage from those closest to us.

I know only too well that playing goalie in hockey requires fortitude. I have already described the fear that goalies experience of giving up bad goals. It takes fortitude to overcome that fear. But there was another challenge that goaltenders from a bygone era once experienced: until the 1960s, goalies used to play without masks or helmets. Granted, the game was played somewhat differently back then. More emphasis was placed on passing and finesse to get the puck to the net rather than on booming slap shots. Still, it is incredible to see photos of goalies from that era sprawling face-first on the ice, diving for loose pucks amid a swirl of flying skates and swinging sticks without the protection of helmets and masks!

The first goalie to wear a mask in a National Hockey League game was Jacques Plante in the 1950s. Playing with the Montreal Canadiens, he took a shot in the face that opened a cut. In those days, teams did not carry a backup goalie on their rosters. If a goalie were injured, he would go to the dressing room, get stitched up, and return to the ice. This time, however, Jacques said he was not going back in unless he could wear the mask that he had begun using during practice. At first, the coach, Toe Blake, refused. His view was the prevailing opinion in those days: besides obstructing a goalie's view, a mask was seen as a sign of weakness or even cowardice. But when Jacques insisted, Toe did not have much choice in the matter, since there was no other goalie available. So, Jacques became the pioneer of the goalie's facemask.

Jacques Plante's courage was twofold. First, he played many years facing flying pucks without a mask. His other example of courage may have been even more difficult. He had to stand up to authority and peer pressure to do something he believed to be right—that is, wear a mask!

THE FORTITUDE OF MARY ELIZABETH LANGE AND OTHER CATHOLIC HEROES

While it may be easy to relate to the examples of fortitude from the world of sports, don't forget the dramatic lives of courage lived by saints, martyrs, and other Catholic heroes. For example, St. Peter and St. Paul had the bravery to go to the heart of the Roman Empire to tell the whole world about the Good News of Jesus Christ. They and many other early Christians were put to death in Rome as a result. My patron saints, St. Thomas More and St. John Fisher, died as martyrs for the faith in sixteenth-century England because they would not agree to King Henry VIII's rejection of the authority of the pope.

An incredible example of fortitude is the story of Mary Elizabeth Lange, who was born into slavery in Haiti in the late 1700s (her exact birthdate is unknown) before fleeing to the United States and settling in Baltimore. She devoutly practiced her Catholic faith, and in 1828, she and three other free black women pronounced vows and established a new religious community, the Oblate Sisters. Think about some of the seemingly insurmountable obstacles Mary Elizabeth faced, not the least of which include the following:

- She and her fellow sisters were black in what was at the time a slaveholding nation.
- She was a woman in a patriarchal society.
- She was a Catholic in a predominantly Protestant country.
- She was a French-speaking immigrant in an English-speaking city.

Like the young David courageously facing Goliath, Mary Elizabeth did not back down from these challenges but instead drew strength and fortitude from her faith in God. Mary Elizabeth and her fellow sisters worked tirelessly to serve black refugees who arrived from Santo Domingo in the Caribbean. She eventually expanded her efforts to provide education to black girls, establishing a school that taught fine arts, music, and the classics as part of the curriculum along with vocational training and religious instruction. In time, the sisters began taking in elderly women and widows and providing care for them. They bravely and tirelessly provided care during a cholera epidemic in Baltimore.

Among the hardships she faced along the way were the deaths and relocations of major benefactors, forcing Mary Elizabeth to provide laundry and ironing services to make ends meet. The archbishop of Baltimore ordered the sisters to disband in the midst of these financial crises, but Mary Elizabeth refused, a bold response to Church authority in any age, let alone in the mid-nineteenth century by a black woman to a white man. The archbishop, to his credit, did not use his authority to disband the sisters even though public opinion was strongly on his side. Meanwhile, Mary Elizabeth was threatened with physical violence, including several incidents when angry mobs knocked down the front door to the convent. On a regular basis, white people who thought it scandalous that black women would wear habits normally worn by white religious women forced the sisters from the sidewalks.

Despite these challenges, Mary Elizabeth and her fellow sisters did not despair but rather continued on courageously to create opportunities for black women. Along the way, they founded an orphanage (tending to the needs of the many war orphans who flooded into Baltimore after the Civil War), provided spiritual direction, created a home for widows, offered Bible classes, did home visits, and even conducted evening classes so that black adults could learn to read and write. All of this was a remarkable testimony to courage by a woman of African and Haitian descent, living in the time and place that she did.

Mary Elizabeth Lange was not alone in her bravery. In United States history, there were many other Catholic religious communities of women pioneers, with little or no money and resources, who braved countless hardships to establish schools, hospitals, and numerous other social institutions, many of which continue to serve today. The earliest of these communities were the Ursuline Sisters, founded by St. Angela Merici in Italy in 1535. The Ursulines were the first Catholic nuns to make the grueling voyage to the New World in 1639, landing in Canada. In 1727, twelve French Ursuline nuns arrived in New Orleans. Today, the Ursuline Academy in New Orleans is the oldest continually operating Catholic school in the United States.

Remember, the Ursulines, and many other communities of religious sisters who followed, established their ministries and institutions during a time when women didn't even have the right to vote and Catholics in general were not very welcome in this country. In their distinctive Catholic garb, they were easy targets for those with anti-Catholic sentiments. Their courageous, compassionate, and tireless efforts, especially during the Civil War when sisters provided much-needed care for soldiers on both sides, went a long way toward allaying Americans' suspicions, fears, and dislikes of Catholics.

Examples of fortitude are not only found in the past or in communities of religious. In my own family, my mother, Veronica Paprocki, has lived a life of great courage. Perhaps her courage in faith was no more evident when as a thirteen-year-old girl she and her younger brother, my Uncle Eugene, went on their own to the parish rectory, rang the doorbell, and asked to be baptized. It seems that their parents, my grandparents, had never had Mom or Uncle Eugene baptized, even though they themselves were Catholic.

My mom had become accustomed to accompanying her best friend, Ramona, to church every Saturday and waiting in the pew while Ramona went to confession. Mom decided that she too wanted to go to confession so that she could experience God's loving mercy and forgiveness in the Sacrament of Penance. So, Mom took it upon herself to become Catholic.

I call Mom an "intentional Catholic" since she sought Baptism on her own initiative. As a result, I think she and many others who embrace the Catholic faith as adults are often more intentional and consciously aware of practicing their faith than are many of us cradle Catholics, who can slip into the routine of being Catholic without consciously pursuing a deeper understanding of what it is that we believe. Yes, to practice the Catholic faith intentionally requires fortitude, especially in an increasingly secular society.

FORTITUDE COMES FROM GOD

It does take special courage to practice our faith. When Tim Tebow publicly expressed his belief in Jesus, many of his opponents and even teammates were critical of him for doing so. Many people, athletes or not, are reluctant to embrace their faith or express their religious beliefs publicly because they fear that being known as a Christian will be a sign of weakness. I think it's just the opposite! It's easy to give in to the peer pressure of living a sinful life, but it takes great fortitude to resist such pressure and have the courage to live a life of virtue.

In William Shakespeare's play *Henry V*, there is a powerful scene preceding the Battle of Agincourt on St. Crispin's Day, October 25, 1415. The English are outnumbered by the French five to one. When King Henry overhears someone wish that some of the unemployed men back in England could have been with them to help them in battle, the king delivers his impassioned address—known as the St. Crispin's Day speech—to his troops, whom he calls his "band of brothers." Roused and inspired by Henry's oratory, the king and his band of brothers go on to victory, despite the overwhelming odds. After the Battle of Agincourt, when it was apparent that the English had been victorious, Henry V praised God and referenced the opening words of Psalm 115: *Non nobis, Domine, non nobis, sed nomine tuo, da Gloriam*, "Not to us. Lord, not to us, but to your name, give the glory."

God is always with us to provide the courage we need. In the Old Testament, Jewish King Hezekiah encouraged his troops to face the invasion of the larger Assyrian army with these words: "Be strong and steadfast; do not be afraid or dismayed because of the king of Assyria and all the throng coming with him. For he has only an arm of flesh, but we have the Lord, our God, to help us and to fight our battles" (2 Chronicles 32:7–8). Scripture makes it clear that fortitude is not a matter of self-reliance but of reliance upon the strength of God, which fuels our courage.

FORTITUDE COMES IN ALL SHAPES AND SIZES

As we live our lives, we don't know when exactly we will need to draw on our courage. It may be in a dramatic situation when our faith is clearly tested. Or we may need this gift of fortitude in more ordinary tasks: taking a test, applying for a job, engaging with a new friend, forgiving an enemy. Situations that require courage may change depending on circumstances of time and place, as well as on the perspective of the person.

Imagine a scene today where the tables are turned from the Jacques Plante–Toe Blake scenario described previously: A goalie says he does not want to use a mask, that it would obscure his vision and cost the team goals. What do you think the coach would say? My guess is that most coaches today would refuse to let such a goalie take the ice, if not out of concern for the goalie's safety, at least out of fear of a lawsuit if the goalie was injured! This change in attitude from a former era to the current day should teach us another lesson about fortitude: Respect how this gift plays out uniquely in the life of each person. For some, the very thought of lacing up skates and stepping on the ice invokes panic. For experienced hockey players who learned to skate at the age of three, that's not even a second thought.

Most people absolutely fear getting up in front of an audience to speak in public. To do so requires digging deep for an inner strength. That was true for me when I first started preaching. But over the years I have preached so many homilies and given so many speeches that I could hardly claim that public speaking requires any great fortitude for me any more.

Fortitude is reaching down deep inside to overcome fear, failures, and frustrations. Just because a certain situation does not invoke fear of failure or frustration for some people does not mean that it doesn't give rise to such reactions for others. We need to keep this in mind when we may not be aware that another person is facing a fearful moment or when we have a dreadful foreboding about something that others seem to take nonchalantly.

The bottom line is that fortitude is not self-reliance but confident trust in God's grace working within us. The cowardly lion in *The Wizard of Oz* wanted the Wizard to give him a heart of courage, not realizing that he already had that virtue within him. Virtues are God's gifts already written on our hearts. People do not develop virtuous hearts on their own initiative, but in response to God's grace and by cultivating the gifts that he has given us. St. Augustine said, "Pray as if everything depended on God, but act as if everything depended on you." This expresses the healthy balance that we need between self-reliance and passively leaving everything in God's hands.

QUOTATION

Do not ask me to give in to this body of mine. I cannot afford it. Between me and my body there needs to be a struggle until death.

—St. Margaret of Cortona

PROMISE

I will recognize the times I hit my own "wall," and I will draw on the fortitude of Jesus, the saints, and . . .

PRAYER

O God, your saints show us what it means to be brave in imitation of your Son, Jesus, who died on the Cross to forgive our sins. Fill us with fortitude to face our fears, frustrations, and failures. May the virtue of courage make us strong and steadfast. When we succeed, may we give glory to your name. We ask this through Christ our Lord. Amen.

STEP 5: FAITH

Success requires confidence, which comes from the Latin words con *and* fide, *meaning "with faith." Winning at life is about having faith in God and in the gifts that he has given you.*

My given name "Thomas" is associated with doubt, the opposite of faith, because of the Apostle Thomas. It was Thomas who was absent when the Risen Jesus appeared to the other Apostles and then doubted that any of the incident even occurred (see Mark 16:14–16; Luke 24:36–48; John 20:19–21).

Perhaps that is one reason why, although I am named Thomas, I have not usually looked to St. Thomas the Apostle as my patron saint, preferring the great English statesman, lawyer, and chancellor of England, St. Thomas More, who died as a martyr to the faith. Likewise, I have always admired St. Thomas Aquinas, the Dominican priest who is probably the Church's greatest theologian. However, in a sense, all of us who are named Thomas walk in the footsteps of the "doubting Apostle." In fact, everyone, regardless of how we are named, can identify with a person who struggled with doubts, since we all must face that challenge at various times and to various degrees in our lives.

In my own life, I have been ordained a priest and a bishop, passed the bar exam, earned a doctoral degree in canon law, completed numerous marathons, and faced more than my fair share of speeding pucks as a goalie. Nevertheless, it might surprise some people to learn that I continue to struggle with doubts every time I face a new challenge. Ironically, I view overcoming doubts as a key to achieving any accomplishment. When I see a goal that seems difficult to reach, rather than shrink from it, I am motivated to confront my doubts and overcome the obstacles that stand in the way of attaining it.

I began thinking this way when I was a young man. When I was in high school and it was time for me to take driver's education, for some reason I thought that driving a car was something beyond my capability. I was afraid to even try. Maybe it was because as a young boy it took me longer than most to learn to ride a bicycle. Once I did learn to ride a bike, I loved it and would ride for miles on the south side of Chicago. Then the same thing happened when it came time to learn how to drive a car. At first, I struggled to get a handle on the intricacies of driving, and I had my doubts that I would pass the test. But instead of shrinking from the challenge, I met it head on. Eventually, I overcame those doubts, learned how to drive, and got my driver's license. Then, like any other teen, I asked my dad for the car every chance I could!

I mentioned in the discussion of step 4 that we need fortitude to overcome the fear of speaking in public. Although I wanted to be a priest for as long as I can remember, my biggest obstacle was coming to grips with the fact that a large part of a priest's duties is preaching. It wasn't that getting up in front of people made me nervous as much as the fact that I was a quiet boy and I doubted that I would have something worthwhile to say to a church full of people. Of course, studying philosophy, theology, scripture, and homiletics helped me to overcome those doubts. Now, I speak so often in public that it's hard to believe that it was ever a concern of mine.

Learning a skill and perfecting it through persistent practice is the way to overcome our self-doubts about performing that skill. However, there is a prior step that is necessary before we can even begin the learning process: First, there must be a leap of faith. We need to believe enough in the possibility of achieving the goal in order to at least make the effort. Faith begins the process of acquiring confidence. Practicing to perfect a skill bolsters one's confidence. As a result, confident ability can carry us to success.

CONFIDENCE AND FAITH GO HAND IN HAND

Shortly after I was appointed Bishop of Springfield in 2010, I received a phone call from the director of the hockey program at one of our high schools, Sacred Heart–Griffin Catholic High School. He said that he had heard about my love of hockey. He also knew that I played goalie, so he invited me to be the goalie coach of the school's club hockey team. I agreed, and I have thoroughly enjoyed my interaction with the players, their parents, and my fellow coaches. As goalie coach, I focus on what's happening in the goalie's head and in his heart. The mechanics of the game are easy to teach and to practice. The mental part is the challenge. If a goalie is distracted by problems at school, distraught about fighting with his girlfriend, or distressed by a lack of confidence, he's not going to be on his best game.

I also have the opportunity to talk to the entire team before games. I leave the game strategy to the other coaches. The primary objective of my pregame talks is to instill confidence in the players. Having confidence is crucial for success in any endeavor. The word "confidence" comes from the Latin words "*con*" and "*fide,*" which mean "with faith." We all need to have faith in God and in ourselves to use the talents and abilities that he gave us. To paraphrase what St. Augustine might have said in a pregame speech to a high school hockey team: "Pray as if everything depends on God. Play the game as if everything depends on you."

Once during practice I asked my goalie if he talks to himself when he's playing. He sheepishly said, "Yes." I said, "That's good!" People think goalies are a little nuts anyway, but self-talk helps build confidence. Ron Hextall, former goalie for the Philadelphia Flyers, used to talk to his goalposts. Okay, that might be a little nuts, but I personally find that, when a player is bearing down on me on a breakaway, it helps when I say to myself, "You can stop this." Talking to yourself can help you face up to and overcome the obstacles of daily life. Any time you face a challenge, tell yourself, "I can do this!"

Confidence, of course, plays an important role in all sports, not just hockey. For example, in running a marathon you've got to believe in your ability to do the training and to finish the race. My track coach used to offer the following advice for doing speed workouts: When you think you're going as fast as you can, you've probably got a little bit more in you. You need to believe that you can do better and then go ahead and make things happen!

THE BIBLICAL HALL OF FAITH

The Bible contains many examples of people who, motivated by faith, confidently accomplished great achievements. In fact, if you would like to read a summary of the faith and some of the Bible's heroes of faith, check out chapter 11 of the Letter to the Hebrews, sometimes called the "faith chapter" of the Bible. I think of this chapter as the "Hall of Faith." It starts by offering a description: "Faith is the realization of what is hoped for and evidence of things not seen" (Hebrews 11:1). Then it lists people of faith and the miraculous results that they realized by placing their faith in God's grace. Here are just a few examples:

- By faith, Abel offered to God a better sacrifice than Cain.
- By faith, Enoch was taken up so that he would not see death.
- By faith, Noah, being warned by God about things not yet seen, prepared an ark for the salvation of his household.
- By faith, Abraham responded to God's call and left his homeland, not knowing where he was going.
- By faith, Sarah received the ability to conceive, even though she was advanced in years.
- By faith, Jacob, as he was dying, blessed each of the sons of Joseph, and worshiped, leaning on the top of his staff.

- By faith, Joseph, when he was dying, made mention of the exodus of the sons of Israel, and gave orders concerning his bones.
- By faith, Moses kept the Passover and the sprinkling of the blood, so that he who destroyed the firstborn would not touch them.
- By faith, the Israelites passed through the Red Sea as though they were passing through dry land; and the Egyptians, when they attempted it, were drowned.
- By faith, the walls of Jericho fell down after they had been encircled for seven days.

The author of Hebrews summarizes the lesson of faith by writing:

> What more shall I say? I have not time to tell of Gideon, Barak, Samson, Jephthah, of David and Samuel and the prophets, who by faith conquered kingdoms, did what was righteous, obtained the promises; they closed the mouths of lions, put out raging fires, escaped the devouring sword; of weakness they were made powerful, became strong in battle, and turned back foreign invaders. (Hebrews 11:32–34)

The bottom line is that the people who placed their faith in God were not disappointed.

Interestingly, the first verse of Hebrews 12 has special application to faith and athletics:

> Therefore, since we are surrounded by so great a cloud of witnesses, let us rid ourselves of every burden and sin that clings to us and persevere in running the race that lies before us while keeping our eyes fixed on Jesus, the leader and perfecter of faith. For the sake of the joy that lay before him he endured the cross, despising its shame, and has taken his seat at the right hand of the throne of God. (Hebrews 12:1)

Those lines really struck home for me, especially one day when I came back from a grueling track workout and used them for prayer.

A little background: I had been in Dallas for a meeting when I decided to go out for a training run. I drove out to the Trinity River, parked my car, and planned to run out three miles, cross a bridge over the river, and run back on the other side. It was a typical day in Texas, sunny and scorching hot. What I didn't know was that it had rained the day before and the banks of the river were muddy. As I ran, the mud began caking up on the bottom of my running shoes. By the time I reached the half-way point at the bridge, the mud on my shoes was so thick that it felt like I had lead weights in my shoes.

I thought the run back to my car was going to be really tough. But the other bank of the river was on higher ground and not so muddy, so I stopped to see if I could scrape the mud off my shoes. To my amazement, the layer of mud easily peeled off each shoe in one piece. I was able to run back normally, feeling much lighter on my feet. When I later prayed the verses from the Letter to the Hebrews, I knew I had just literally lived out the image: "Let us rid ourselves of every burden and sin that clings to us and persevere in running."

My prayer went on to reflect on how sin weighs us down and makes life so difficult that sometimes it is barely possible to keep going. When we go to confession and receive God's forgiveness, it is like peeling off a layer of mud that weighs us down. When freed by God's merciful love, we are freed of the burden of sin and can persevere with our eyes fixed on Jesus in running the course of our lives toward our goal: life with Christ in God's Kingdom!

ATHLETES WHO SHARE PUBLIC WITNESS TO THEIR FAITH

I am chairman of the bishop's advisory board for a group called "Catholic Athletes for Christ." The group's membership includes professional and amateur athletes from all of the major sports. Its mission is to serve Catholic athletes and share the Gospel of Christ in and through athletics. We try to minister to Catholic athletes, coaches, and staff in the practice of their faith. We encourage these same people to use the unique platform given to them to reach the world for Jesus and his Church. This group was formed in response to the call of Blessed Pope John Paul II to evangelize the world of sports. At a Mass to celebrate sports held in Rome's olympic stadium on a Sunday in 2000, Pope John Paul II said, "Every Christian is called to become a strong athlete of Christ, that is, a faithful and courageous witness to his Gospel."

I have met with players and coaches from across the spectrum of sports. One of the most inspiring people I have met is former big-league catcher Mike Piazza. When he first entered professional baseball, 1,389 players were picked before him. He was only drafted in the sixty-second round as a favor to Tom Lasorda, the manager of the Dodgers and Mike's godfather. Mike overcame many obstacles to become regarded as the best-hitting catcher in major-league history. His 397 homeruns are an all-time record for catchers. Mike is a devout Catholic and is featured in *Champions of Faith*, a documentary exploring the intersection of Catholic religious faith and sports. Mike never hesitates speaking out about the importance of faith in his life and how faith played such an important role in his career in baseball:

> I truly believe my whole professional career was a blessing from God. And it's been a great gift. I know I worked hard, and you have to apply yourself, but I still feel that you have to have a lot of blessings from above. And anybody who plays this game, you have to be very spiritual, because it's very frustrating at times.

Mike Piazza also shares how his faith had practical applications to playing the game on a daily basis:

> As a player, you have to believe. I had to believe every day when I got in that batter's box good things were going to happen. I couldn't go up there thinking, "Oh, I'm going to strike out. Or I'm going to hit into a double play." Or even if I was 0 for 20, I had to believe that that twenty-first time I was going to get that hit.

Rebecca Dussault is another member of the athlete's advisory board. She competed for the US Olympic team in cross-country skiing in the 2006 winter games in Turin, Italy. Among her ambitions is to live a life of heroic virtue to become a saint. In one of her witness talks she said, "My truest love of all is the Lord Jesus Christ and his holy Catholic Church. My faith is the most important thing in my life."

One of Rebecca's heroes was coincidentally a Turin native, Blessed Pier Giorgio Frassati. Born in 1901, Pier was known for giving away his money and helping the poor. Once, in Rome, he stood up to the police when they brutally assaulted a protestor at a rally. Pier was also an active outdoorsman. He especially loved to ski. When Rebecca raced in the Olympics she marked her skis with Pier's favorite quotation: "To live without faith, without patrimony to defend, without a steady struggle for truth, that is not living but existing."

Pier Giorgio Frassati died at the young age of twenty-four from the effects of polio and has since become a model for lay people and athletes all over the world. Beatified in 1990 by Pope John Paul II and named "the Man of the Eight Beatitudes," Giorgio teaches us that holiness can be applied in all aspects of life, including athletics. He is known as the "saint on skis."

Catholic Athletes for Christ also has a speakers' bureau. Joe Lombardi, the quarterback coach for the New Orleans Saints and grandson of the legendary coach Vince Lombardi, has spoken to our Knights of Columbus in the Diocese of Springfield. Joe is the father of five children, and he follows his grandfather's credo that the three things that matter most in life are faith, family, and football—"and definitely in that order."

A complete list of speakers, along with several motivational words connecting faith with sports can be found at the Athletes for Christ website: www.catholicathletesforchrist.com. Check it out!

MORE ABOUT THE MEANING OF FAITH

Faith is crucial both in sports and in life. Imagine if a goalie didn't have faith in the defensemen to deflect some shots in front of him. It would make for a long game to have to go it alone. Too often people just think of faith as a feeling. Faith is not a blind leap. We are to know in whom we are putting our faith. The word "theology" comes from two Greek words *theo* and *logos,* which mean "God" and "the study of." That's why we study our faith, to know more about God and how we are to live. Theology, then, provides us with words about God to understand him better. Ultimately, faith is the acceptance of Jesus Christ and his Gospel message. Christians put their faith in Jesus.

We also put our faith in others who act in Jesus' name and in his place. Think about parents who leave their children under the care of a babysitter. They expect that the babysitter will take their place for the time that they are away. The babysitter will feed the children, console them if they are upset, and insist that they follow the family rules.

As we grow up, there are many other people that we grow to trust, both for the longterm and for shorter periods of time. This was my experience when I visited countries like Russia, China, and Turkey, where I didn't know the language or where I was going. So I put my trust in a tour guide to translate and show us around. I didn't put trust in just anyone on the street; our tour guide was recommended and had credentials. Likewise, parents don't just grab anyone off the street to watch their children. They choose a babysitter only after they thoroughly check references. The message here is a simple one: Only trust those whose trust is warranted by their position and merits.

In the Catholic Church, the ordination of deacons, priests, and bishops is a way of certifying that a person has the proper credentials to pass on the faith. We call this "apostolic succession." Through the laying on of hands from Jesus himself to succeeding generations of bishops who are in union with the bishop of Rome, the pope, the Church is saying that you can trust these religious leaders to lead you to Jesus and the truth. In turn, the Church calls many others to assist the bishop in passing on the faith. Priests, who share in the Sacrament of Holy Orders, have a special role. Religious brothers and sisters, lay ecclesial ministers, catechetical leaders and catechists, and teachers at Catholic schools and universities are just some of the baptized who are called to assist the bishops in authentically proclaiming the Gospel of Jesus Christ. All Catholics, by virtue of their Baptism, are also charged with sharing the

Catholic faith with others.

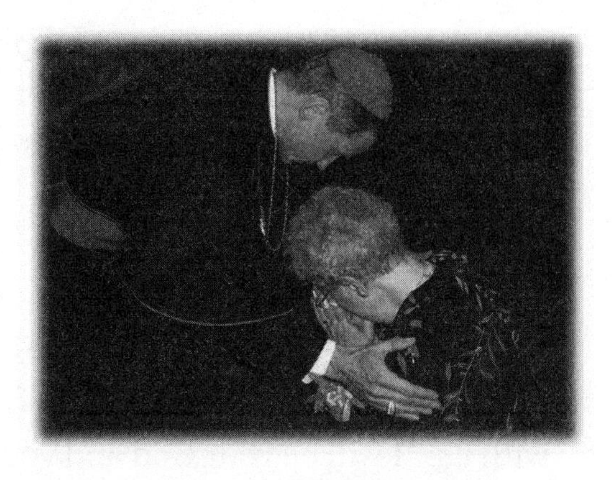

To be a trusted leader with credentials, one must properly exercise the power of authority. Leaders must be trustworthy. Never was this more evident to me than when it was revealed in the early 1990s that some priests had breached the trust placed in them by abusing minors. At the time, I was chancellor of the Archdiocese of Chicago, working under the leadership of Cardinal Joseph Bernardin. Dealing with the issue of clergy sex abuse was not and is not easy. However, like a goalie determined to protect the goal line, I chose not to duck this issue and instead met it head on, with confidence that God would lead us through this ordeal and bring healing and a restoration of trust. I have no doubt that he will do so. We realized that it was crucial for Church leadership to reestablish trust after this terrible breach. But how to do so?

In 1992, before the clergy sex-abuse crisis exploded both nationally and eventually internationally, we had put in place in the Archdiocese of Chicago policies and procedures for addressing clerical sexual misconduct with minors. These policies and procedures became a model which many other dioceses adopted. Today, the Church continues to work to reestablish her trust after this terrible breach.

GOD IS FAITHFUL

Yes, God *is* faithful. God keeps his promises to us. We call God's promise a *covenant*. God made this covenant with us: "I will be your God and you will be my people." This promise is repeated throughout the Bible from the very first book, Genesis, to the final book in the New Testament, the Book of Revelation. Despite our sins and failures and our turning away from him, God has never broken that promise. Ultimately, God has shown us what it means to be perfectly faithful. As we strive to live lives of holiness, we can draw on God's own grace to truly live as people of faith.

St. Francis de Sales, appointed Bishop of Geneva in 1602, often used the phrase "May God give us this grace," to end his sermons and writings. In this way he let his listeners and readers know that, in the end, nothing is possible without God's grace and everything is possible only with God's grace. Several years ago, after reading St. Francis de Sales's book, *Introduction to the Devout Life,* and some of his sermons, I decided that I would end my homilies in the same way. I also conclude the biweekly column that I write for our diocesan newspaper, the *Catholic Times*, with those words. After all, anything I say or write will have no effect on my listeners or readers unless God imbues their hearts with the grace needed to take those words to heart and put them into practice in their lives.

May God give us this grace. Amen.

QUOTATION

The disbelief of Thomas has done more for our faith than the faith of the other disciples. As he touches Christ and is won over to belief, every dobut is cast aside and our faith is strengthened.

—St. Gregory the Great

PROMISE

I will recognize times of doubt and will look for ways to believe by . . .

PRAYER

O God, you freely give the gift of faith, the assurance of things hoped for, the conviction of things not seen. May your grace guide our intellect and will so that we may be faithful: faithful to you, faithful to ourselves, faithful to everyone. Give us confidence to trust in your gifts to guide us to the achievement of our goals. We ask this through Christ our Lord. Amen.

STEP 6: FAMILY

Family life is the first team sport. How we work together and play together as a family will teach us lessons that will last a lifetime.

If you get a chance to go to a Chicago Blackhawks' hockey game at the United Center, you will receive a lesson in the team's history. Even before you enter the "Madhouse on Madison," you are greeted with statues honoring Blackhawks greats Bobby Hull and Stan Mikita (not far, of course, from the statue of Chicago Bulls legend Michael Jordan).

Once inside, your eyes are drawn to the banners hanging from the rafters that bear the numbers of Blackhawks who have had those numbers retired. Besides Bobby and Stan, Tony Esposito, Glenn Hall, Keith Magnuson, and Pierre Pilote all have retired jerseys.

Nearby, you will glance at the banners indicating the too few but still sweet Stanley Cup championships: 1935, 1938, 1961, and 2010.

Shortly before the game begins, an inspiring video is shown to stir up the crowd. Over the course of a few minutes, you and the other fans see a rapid-fire stream of images that tell the story of the team's stars from the past, whose strength, speed, and courage epitomize what it means to proudly wear the Blackhawks' famous Indian-head logo. Finally, with the crowd whipped into a frenzy, the present-day Blackhawks take the ice to thunderous applause. The message is clear: This current roster has to live up to an illustrious legacy and preserve the honor of a proud name.

Growing up, I also had to live up to an illustrious legacy and preserve the honor of a proud name. Being a Paprocki was demanding. The Paprocki name stood for something in our Little Village community on the near-west side of Chicago. Paprocki Pharmacy was a bedrock business in the community since it opened in 1919. My grandparents were pillars of both the local neighborhood and of our parish, St. Casimir's. My own parents were well-respected members of that same parish, leading and participating in numerous organizations and ministries. I was proud to bear the Paprocki family name, and I continue to take pride in it. At the same time, living up to that name was a great responsibility.

In Baptism, we inherit another family name aside from our family of origin. We are named “Christian.” To be a Christian is literally to be one who is “like Christ.” How can we possibly live up to that name? For starters, we look to our faith heritage. Just as the Chicago Blackhawks invoke their legacy before the start of every home game, we, too, look to our forefathers and foremothers in faith.

In fact, scripture reminds us that we belong to a family of faith reaching back many generations. The genealogies we often skip over in the Old Testament (for example, in Exodus 7:14–27) are in fact quite significant. These seemingly endless lists of ancestors reminded the Jewish people that they belonged to a family and that this family had a name to live up to—the name of God. Heroes like Abraham, Sarah, Jacob, Joseph, Moses, Ruth, Esther, David, and Solomon also teach us what it means to belong to the family that bears God’s name. In the New Testament genealogies (see Matthew 1:1–17 and Luke 3:23–38), we find a new set of heroes who show us what it means to live up to the name “Christian.”

It is the names of these biblical heroes and many other saints that we invoke in the Litany of Saints when anyone approaches the waters of Baptism. The message is clear: Baptism incorporates us into a family. The family is our Church.

SCHOOLED IN FAMILY AND FAITH

Growing up in the Paprocki family, I never would have dreamt that people would one day refer to me as the "holy goalie." I was not particularly athletic as a youth. In pickup games of softball or basketball, I was usually the last to be chosen. I got used to it, so I guess I never had great expectations for personal achievements in sports. Playing various games was just a way to have fun and spend time with family and friends.

There were many opportunities for me to participate in team sports as a kid. I come from a big family, the third of nine children. The oldest and the youngest are girls, with seven boys in between. All we had to do was get a few friends from the neighborhood, and we could easily field two teams for just about any sport.

Hockey was our favorite sport. In order to play it, we took to our apartment building's long, narrow, dirty, dank basement that was filled with coal dust, mold, and mildew—not to mention a few varieties of pests. We dubbed it the "Cermak Coliseum" since it was nestled on the corner of Cermak Road and Sacramento Avenue. We took our sticks and plastic pucks indoors and made "nets" out of discarded boxes from the drug store. We painted lines and goalie creases on the floor, pinned up an old forty-eight-star flag on the door (for the national anthem, of course), and began a hockey league, inviting kids from all over the neighborhood to join us.

The Cermak Coliseum was our attempt to create a miniature version of the great arenas where the National Hockey League played. It was our own sanctuary of sports, and we had great times in our basement-turned-arena. My siblings and I and lots of other kids from the neighborhood were "schooled" in the ways of hockey—not to mention teamwork, cooperation, and friendship—at the Cermak Coliseum.

When it comes to growing in faith, we also need schooling, and there is no better place for that to happen than in the family. The family is like the Cermak Coliseum in a couple of ways. The Church refers to the family as the “domestic church”—a miniature version of the larger Church that we experience in our parishes, dioceses, and in the world. Also, Catholic families are the place where young people are schooled, not in the world of sports, but in a life of faith. I can say without a doubt that the Paprocki home was indeed a domestic church. In fact, while I was being schooled in the Cermak Coliseum in the art of being a goalie, I was simultaneously being schooled by my family—my parents, grandparents, aunts and uncles, siblings—in the art of being holy.

You might even say that I started working on the “holy” part of what would eventually become my moniker before I got really interested in the “goalie” aspect of it. Mom says that I was about four years old when I started talking about wanting to be a priest. I used to “play Mass” using the china closet built into the dining-room wall as my altar (this was in the early 1960s before altars were turned around to face the congregation).

At first I wore “vestments” my mom made for me out of old dish towels. Later on, my mom actually ordered a set of “play vestments” specifically designed for children, which she saw advertised in a Catholic magazine. I used oyster crackers for hosts and grape juice instead of wine. Again, it helped being from a big family. To add to the atmosphere, my older sister, Ramona, dressed as a nun, and my brothers served as altar boys.

Kids from the neighborhood (often the same ones who came to play hockey) were the congregation. We even took up a collection, but we used *Monopoly* money instead of real cash!

I have to admit, though, that holiness was not always my primary motivation for playing Mass. It was also a good way to get out of doing chores around the house. I remember one time my brother Jim was washing the windows of our apartment, which was on the second floor above our drug store. Jim would open the window and sit on the ledge so he could wash the glass on the outside as well as the inside. That seemed way too dangerous for me, so I would get out of doing that by playing Mass instead. Seeing this, Jim complained to Mom, "Why doesn't Tommy help me wash the windows?" I responded, "I'm praying so you won't fall out the window!" That seemed to work, since Mom let me continue to play Mass.

Both of my parents played a significant role in my growth in holiness. I already related my Mom's courageous story of seeking out her own Baptism. My dad also played a significant role in my interest in priesthood. Dad was once a seminarian himself, graduating in 1939 from Chicago's high school seminary, Quigley Preparatory. He even went for one year to the Archdiocese of Chicago's major seminary in Mundelein, Illinois, known then as St. Mary of the Lake Seminary. It was there that Dad realized that God wasn't calling him to be a priest. Although Dad didn't become a priest, he was a model of holiness, setting an example of what it meant to:

- work hard,
- love selflessly,
- serve others,
- be humble, patient, and forgiving,
- be a man of prayer, and
- faithfully participate in the life of the Church.

Looking back at my family life, I can see that sports and faith were important aspects of those formative years. I never saw them as separate realities. Both were part and parcel of who I was and who I was becoming. As a result, I came to recognize that sports and faith share some key elements in common.

While some sports, such as triathlons and marathons, focus on individual performance to accomplish one's goals, team sports like baseball, football, basketball, hockey, and soccer rely on a group of people working and sticking together to achieve success. Within these team sports, individual achievement still plays a key role, but victory usually goes to the team whose members, not only help to complement each other's strengths and compensate for their weaknesses, but also get along well enough to forge a team spirit and camaraderie necessary for fostering a winning attitude.

FAITH IS A TEAM EFFORT

Just as individual skills blend together in team play for athletic success, the same is true in the world of faith. There is obviously a personal aspect to spirituality in terms of one's interior prayer life and relationship with God. Unfortunately, too many people stop there, especially in our highly individualistic culture. Many people today describe themselves as "spiritual, but not religious," meaning they want no part of organized religion.

In fact, this narrow, one-to-one relationship between a person and God is not the way of the Judeo-Christian tradition, which places a premium on individuals joining together to pray, support, and strengthen each other. It is significant that the word "religion" comes from the Latin words *re* and *legio*, which mean "to bind together again." The word "legion" derives from the same Latin root. A legion is a group that bands together for a common cause. Religion binds its members to each other and ultimately to God. Why is that important? We can accomplish so much more working together than we could ever do individually.

Just as with sports, teamwork is essential for life in general, and in particular for our faith life. Yet many people strangely embrace the "lone ranger" mentality of faith. They name several reasons they are put off by organized religion, from boredom to saying they do not want to belong to a Church of sinners. (In fact, the Church *is* made up of sinners! Forgiven sinners!) However, when it comes to our relationship with God, it is so much more difficult, if not impossible, to nurture and sustain that relationship alone as opposed to binding ourselves to one another in order to draw strength from each other. It's easy to snap a single twig, but if you bind a bunch of twigs together, they're almost impossible to break. Similarly, if we try to face the forces of evil alone, the devil can snap us like a twig, but if we are part of a team—a family bonded by the glue of God's grace—we become an impenetrable force for good.

God is relational; the Blessed Trinity is a communion of Three Persons. Jesus himself did not intend for people to form a relationship with God on their own. He said to St. Peter: "You are Peter, and upon this rock I will build my church, and the gates of the netherworld shall not prevail against it" (Matthew 16:18). Calling Peter "rock" was a very intentional play on words. The New Testament was written mainly in Greek. The name Peter in Greek is *Petros*, and the Greek word for rock is *petra*. St. Peter was also known as *Cephas*, the word for "rock" in Aramaic, which Jesus spoke. Thus, what Jesus actually said to Peter in Aramaic was: "You are Rock and on this very rock I will build my Church." Jesus was being very clear—he was not sharing a private philosophy of life. He gave us a community of faith to allow us to pray, worship, and meditate on our relationship with God with others.

In the twelfth century, Blessed Isaac of Stella, the abbot of a Cistercian community of monks, described this relationship between Christ and the Church. In a sermon which is reprinted in the Church's Liturgy of the Hours, Blessed Isaac said,

> The Church is incapable of forgiving any sin without Christ, and Christ is unwilling to forgive any sin without the Church. The Church cannot forgive the sin of one who has not repented, who has not been touched by Christ; Christ will not forgive the sin of one who despises the Church.

In other words, the Church has no authority to forgive without Christ's grace, yet when Christ gave that authority to the Church he made it clear that one cannot separate him from the Church since the Church is the very Body of Christ.

SPORTS AND FAMILY LIFE TEACH LESSONS ABOUT RESPECT AND AUTHORITY

There was no question in the Paprocki family about who had authority: Mom and Dad. While both were gentle and loving parents, they assumed the role of authority without hesitation and commanded respect. The fourth commandment, "Honor your father and mother," addresses the importance of respect that is due to rightful authority. It's interesting to note, however, that the *Catechism of the Catholic Church* expands upon this notion of authority to beyond parents, reminding us to show respect for all legitimate authority, including police officers, teachers, and political leaders. All aspects of respect for authority begin in the family.

Fr. Robert Barron, author and producer of the groundbreaking book and film series *Catholicism*, explains a helpful approach to understanding authority. Fr. Barron describes what he calls the "designated authority" of an umpire in a baseball game. When an umpire calls a runner "out," the runner is out. The runner is still out even if every player on both teams, all of the fans in attendance, and even the millions watching the game on television can see that the runner was really safe. The reason that the umpire's decision is the only one that matters is because he has been designated as the authority to make that call final. There is no video review of an umpire's calls (at least for now) regarding whether a runner is safe or out. This doesn't mean that umpires (or referees, police officers, or parents) are perfect. They do make mistakes. However, as designated and legitimate authorities, they are worthy and deserving of our respect.

Another person who understands the role of authority is Kerry Fraser, who was a National Hockey League referee for thirty years. I have gotten to know Kerry Fraser personally through Catholic Athletes for Christ. He officiated more than two thousand games from 1980 to 2010 and wrote a book about his experiences called *The Final Call.* Kerry is a Catholic who values his faith and family, with hockey coming in a solid third place.

Kerry tells an interesting story about a game that he officiated at the United Center on October 12, 2009, between the Blackhawks and the Calgary Flames. It happens that my brother Joe and I were in attendance at that game, thanks to Kerry getting tickets for us. The game started out as a nightmare for the Blackhawks and their fans. The Flames scored five goals in four and a half minutes in the first period to jump out to a 5–0 lead. Joe and I were tempted to leave, but we decided to stick around just because we love watching hockey so much and we wanted to thank Kerry for the tickets in person after the game. We're glad we did stay, but I'll get to the reason why in a moment.

Shortly after the Blackhawks scored a goal in the second period to make it 5–1, Kerry Fraser called a penalty for goaltender interference on the Blackhawks' Troy Brouwer when he charged hard to the Calgary goal and knocked the Flames' goalie Mikka Kiprusoff into the net. Kerry describes what happened next:

> Fearing their comeback effort might be thwarted by the penalty, the young captain, Jonathan Toews, protested the call vociferously with an attitude I had not seen from him since he had arrived in the league. He got a little fatherly attitude back when I said, "Son, I was calling that a penalty in this league when you were in diapers, so I think you better be a little more respectful and pick your spots when and how to complain." The very next stoppage in play Jonathan came to me and apologized for his conduct and admitted he had crossed the line. This young star, mature beyond his years, has not only earned the respect of all his teammates, but on this particular night from the most senior referee in the NHL.

Obviously Joe and I were not aware of that conversation at the time, but reading about it later told me a lot about Jonathan Toews and his respect for authority.

This attitude should be a prerequisite for anyone who plays a sport and especially for those who wear the "C" on their shirts that indicates their leadership role as captain.

Oh, and there was something else that happened that made us happy that we stuck around. The Blackhawks scored four more goals to tie the game, and then won it twenty-six seconds into overtime!

MORE ABOUT FAITH AND FAMILY IN THE WORLD OF SPORTS

I have to share one more part of the story about the Blackhawks' big comeback in the game described in the previous section.

The night before that game I was at a restaurant in Chicago with folks from Catholic Athletes for Christ and Sports Faith International when I recognized the coach of the Calgary Flames, Brent Sutter, and his staff sitting at the table next to mine. I went over to introduce myself and say hello. I told Coach Sutter that I would be at the game the next night, but I would be rooting for the Blackhawks. I also told him that I would say a prayer of blessing for the Calgary Flames that would be good in any game except for those against the Blackhawks. Coach Sutter and his staff laughed. I think they thought I was kidding. When the Flames jumped out to a 5–0 lead, I wondered if Coach Sutter was thinking that the bishop got his blessing all wrong. I was picturing him and his staff *really* having a good laugh at my expense. By the end of the game, I don't think they were laughing anymore!

By the way, Brent Sutter is from another great hockey family with seven sons, just like the Paprocki family, except for one main difference: six of the seven Sutter brothers played in the National Hockey League! Brent's brother Darryl won the Stanley Cup as coach of the Los Angeles Kings in 2012. But there is a lesser-known fact about Darryl Sutter that makes him a real winner. In 1995, right in the middle of the season, Darryl unexpectedly quit what he called his "dream job" as coach of the Blackhawks. He wanted to help take care of his son Chris, who was born with Down syndrome. Darryl Sutter moved his family back to their farm in Alberta, Canada, where his primary job became driving Chris to therapy sessions three times a week, fifty miles each way. Chris Sutter graduated from high school in June 2012, the same month that his dad won the Stanley Cup with the Kings. I have a feeling that Darryl Sutter feels just as proud of his son Chris as he does about that Stanley Cup!

Blackhawk Hall of Famer Stan Mikita shares another story connecting family with sports in his book *Forever a Blackhawk*. He tells how the influence of his family helped him to win the Lady Byng Trophy, the league's sportsmanship award given to the player with the least penalty minutes. This was surprising because in his early years in the NHL, Stan Mikita was among the most penalized players in the league.

Then, one time after returning home from a road trip, Stan's wife, Jill, told him that their young daughter Meg wondered about why her dad seemed to "always sit by himself" (in the penalty box). Jill suggested that Meg ask her father and get the answer right from his own words. So, when Stan walked through the door, Meg put the same question to him. Stan recalls that her question made him stop and think, "If our baby daughter sees this and feels something is wrong, maybe I was spending too much time serving penalties for my own good and the good of the team." Stan decided then and there that it was time to change his game. He went from 154 penalty minutes in 1964–65 to fifty-eight penalty minutes the following season, and then to twelve minutes and fourteen minutes in the years that he won the Lady Byng Trophy. Stan made quite a transformation in sportsmanship, inspired by his daughter!

Earlier I mentioned Sports Faith International. The founder and chairman of Sports Faith International is Patrick McCaskey, owner of the Chicago Bears. Patrick is the grandson of the late George Halas, the original "Papa Bear" and one of the founding members of the NFL. Sports Faith International is an organization that collects powerful faith testimonies from athletes and uses them to inspire others to live out their faith. Each year Sports Faith International inducts extraordinary athletes, coaches, and teams into its hall of fame. Prior to the induction ceremony at Halas Hall, the Bears' practice facility in Lake Forest, Illinois, there is a Mass, which I have been privileged to celebrate.

Patrick McCaskey is another outstanding example of someone who brings the worlds of sports, faith, and family together. In his book, *Bear with Me: A Family History of George Halas and the Chicago Bears*, Patrick has a chapter called "Growing Up in a Football Family," in which he describes what the family routine was on game days when the Bears were playing at home:

> On many childhood Sundays, it didn't matter what time we got up, as long as we were ready to leave at 7:45 a.m. After all, Mass started at 8:00, and it wouldn't do anybody good to miss a golden moment. In order to meet the first of many deadlines on those glorious days, my mother was on everybody's back to get up and get going. Through the grace of God, no doubt, my seven brothers, my three sisters, my parents, and I managed to pile into both family cars and get to church on time.

After going home for a big family breakfast, they would all climb back into the family cars for the ride to Wrigley Field:

> With God on our side, the hour-long journey passed safely as we prayed the family rosary and offered it for a Bears victory. Between the start of the game at 1:05 p.m. and the final gun at approximately 4:00, there passed my father's outrage at bad officiating, my mother's tears, and my unsuccessful attempts to escape from the whole scene.
>
> We managed to arrive home in time for 6:00 p.m. dinner. My father would finish the grace with a special plea for the Lord to "please convert the Russians." The prayers would end just in time for the 6:15 sports broadcast on WGN radio.

The family would spend the rest of the evening relaxing before watching the highlights of the game on the 10:00 p.m. news. Then, according to Patrick, their dad "called the final play of the day: 'Go right up the hill. Brush your teeth and say your prayers.'"

What I find most fascinating about this account of game day in a famous football family is how prayer punctuated their whole day. I have met Patrick's mother, Mrs. Virginia McCaskey, and she is a very devout Catholic, but it is very significant in Patrick's telling of the story that it was their father who was leading the prayers. Too many people think that religion is only for women. In fact, I once asked a hockey coach if their team had a chaplain, and he explained that they didn't, because many hockey players consider religion a "sign of weakness."

This could not be farther from the truth. Living a Christian life requires a great deal of courage and strength in order to face the temptations and evils of the world and remain steadfast in the face of oppression and persecution. Apparently the Bears organization believes that too, since, to this day, they have a team chaplain who often attends practice, listens to the players' problems (and sometimes confessions), and celebrates Mass for them.

THE MODEL FAMILY

The epitome of family life is the Holy Family: Jesus, Mary, and Joseph. The Bible doesn't say too much about Joseph, but what it does say is significant. Joseph protected his family from danger, taking them into exile in Egypt away from the deadly threats of King Herod. He was a law-abiding citizen who complied with the requirements of both Jewish law and Roman law. He took Jesus to the Temple to pray and to discuss the scriptures. Joseph taught Jesus how to be a carpenter.

Likewise, there is no better example of motherhood than the Blessed Mother, Mary. The Bible tells us that she was there throughout Jesus' life, even at the foot of the Cross where she took him into her arms and watched him die. Later, Mary was present with her son's disciples when the Holy Spirit came to them at Pentecost.

All family members—parents and children alike—would do well to imitate the ideals of Jesus, Mary, and Joseph, the Holy Family.

One final thought about the Paprocki family. As if it wasn't large enough with nine children and numerous aunts, uncles, and cousins, my parents saw fit to teach us to refer to a number of other people as "Aunt" or "Uncle." As I grew older, I discovered that these people were not related to us at all but were to be treated as family members. My parents followed the example of Jesus, who expanded his notion of family to include all those who do the will of his Father. As those who bear the name Christian, we, too, are called to expand our notion of family to include all of God's children who are made in his image and likeness.

QUOTATION

The Church is like a great ship being pounded by the waves of life's different stresses. Our duty is not to abandon ship, but to keep her on course.

—St. Boniface

PROMISE

My loyalty to my family and my Church knows no bounds. I am confident when their authority is tested I will . . .

PRAYER

O God, you give us the Holy Family as the model of family life. Jesus, Mary, and Joseph show us the way to holiness in our families and in our homes. May we follow their example, that by praying together we may stay together in the unity of your love. We ask this through Christ our Lord. Amen.

STEP 7: FRIENDSHIP

Participating in sports is a great way to make friends, and to learn how to work together and rely on each other through thick and thin.

At a retreat for major-league baseball players in Malibu, California, five-time all-star Mike Sweeney gave a talk called "Stealing Home," in which he used the analogy of the baseball diamond to describe how we get to heaven. He said that we start out at home as a child of God. As we get older and head from first base to second base, many of us have moved to a point far from where we started, but the goal is always to round third and come back home to God.

Mike talked about the important role of teammates and friends in successfully reaching home. He then referred to a little-known epitaph on the headstone of the legendary and notorious Billy the Kid. Interestingly enough, Billy the Kid's headstone is inscribed with the word "PALS," in reference to Billy and his best friends, Tom O'Folliard and Charlie Bowdre. "Pals to the end" is what the buddies used to say. In fact, after Billy the Kid's original grave was repeatedly despoiled by souvenir hunters, his body was moved to Fort Sumner where he was buried with these two best friends. Mike Sweeney used the PALS inscription from Billy the Kid's headstone as an acronym to describe the essentials of friendship:

- *"P" is for partnership.* Friendship involves a partnership based on mutuality and reciprocity. That does not mean that friends keep score. Friendship is not a strict tit for tat, *quid pro quo*, you scratch my back and I'll scratch yours. Friendship is a gift marked by spontaneous care and a genuine affection for the other person. On the other hand, if the friendly sentiment is a one-way street, the relationship is not exactly a partnership and probably won't last very long. We read in the Letter to the Hebrews, "Encourage yourselves daily. . . . We have become partners of Christ only if we hold the beginning of the reality firm until the end" (Hebrews 3:13).
- *"A" is for accountability.* Mike Sweeney says that as a baseball player he always made sure that he had an "accountability partner." By this he meant that he would talk to one, two, or three teammates on a regular basis, even weekly, to let each other know

how things were going and to hold themselves accountable to a virtuous life by honestly talking about their daily activities. As Mike put it, "I want my teammates to help me to be the person I want to be."

- *"L" is for love of God and love of neighbor.* True friendship is witnessed by a person's genuine love of God and love of neighbor. Many friendships (especially friendships between males) can be challenged by the inhibition to express affection. However, consider that sports teams with the strongest team spirit are the ones where there is a strong bond of connection between teammates. This bond doesn't necessarily have to be expressed with a lot of hugging and sentimental expressions, but there is an honesty and openness in communication and a tangible sense of a commitment to each other that would go so far as for one to die for one's friend. That is why some of the strongest bonds of friendship emerge from military experiences where soldiers are literally willing to lay down their lives for their comrades. As Jesus said, "No one has greater love than this, to lay down one's life for one's friends" (John 15:13).
- *"S" is for security.* An interesting study that was published in the *Journal of Experimental Social Psychology* provides evidence that friendships build a sense of security. In the study, participants stood at the base of a steep hill and were asked to guess how difficult it would be to climb. Researchers

report that those participants who stood together with a friend estimated the climb to be less difficult than those who stood alone. Knowing that we can count on our friends enables us to live with a sense of security in our daily lives.

Another recent study at the University of Alberta showed how friendship and sports has a correlating relationship. It detailed how children's confidence in their own athletic ability is closely tied with how happy and satisfied they are with the number and kinds of friends they have. It turns out that children with low athletic confidence indicated that they were lonely at school while those with higher athletic confidence indicated greater satisfaction with their friendships. The research suggests that giving children even a minimal amount of athletic involvement can result in improvement in their social life, in particular with regard to friendships.

PARTNERS AND FRIENDS

The world of sports has given us many famous personal rivalries over the years, including classics like Bird and Johnson, Navratilova and Evert, and Federer and Nadal. By the same token, it has also given us many famous partnerships: Stockton and Malone, Montana and Rice, Venus and Serena, and my favorites, Hull and Mikita.

Many of these great partnerships transcended sports and grew into true, lasting friendships.

Bobby Hull and Stan Mikita were teammates on the 1961 Blackhawks Stanley Cup championship team. They were to that team what Jonathan Toews and Patrick Kane were to the 2010 Blackhawks Stanley Cup championship team. Years later, when Blackhawks President John McDonough invited Stan Mikita to be a team ambassador, Stan said, "Let me call Bobby." Stan wasn't going to do this without his friend Bobby Hull, with whom he had shared a friendship since their days in junior hockey. Friendships formed in the world of sports often last a lifetime. Teammates who look out for one another in the playing arena also do so in life.

I have been close friends with some of my current hockey teammates since we played floor hockey together in college. Many of them (and now their children) still get together for floor hockey, followed by pizza and socializing. I have attended or presided at their weddings, baptized their children, and buried their relatives. My teammates on the Lawyers Hockey Team that I have played on since 1997 are not just fellow athletes that skate on the ice together; we are friends who help each other out in times of need.

Team sports have obvious camaraderie, but solidarity and support are important in individual sports too. Running is a good example. I trained for my first

marathon by myself, which was really tough. In the marathon itself, my brother Allen and I ran side by side the entire 26.2 miles. Doing so gave strength to both of us to finish. The following year I joined the Chicago Area Runners Association and trained with a pace group in their marathon-training program. I took a half hour off my time that year and another half hour off the next year so that I qualified for the Boston Marathon. I sincerely doubt that I could have done that if I hadn't trained with the group. In the Book of Ecclesiastes, we read, "Two are better than one. . . . If the one falls, the other will lift up his companion. Woe to the solitary man! For if he should fall, he has no one to lift him up" (Ecclesiastes 4:9–10).

TRUE FRIENDSHIPS INSPIRE US

True friendships are relatively rare, not like countless people that we "friend" on Facebook! We can usually count our true friends on one hand, because true friends are those few who truly inspire us. Back in the twelfth century, a Scottish Cistercian monk, Aelred of Rievaulx, identified three types of friends.

- He called the first type of friends *carnal*, meaning that the only real bond shared is a mutual pursuit of some vice (e.g., gangs, crime rings).
- The second type of friendship he called *worldly*, meaning that these friends latch on to one another hoping to gain something from the friendship (e.g., the "friends" who surface when one wins the lottery).
- Finally, Aelred refers to the third type of friends as *spiritual*, meaning that these friends have one goal in mind: the well-being of the other. Spiritual friends share common morals and beliefs and seek to help one another lead lives of holiness. These are friends who stand with us during good times and bad.

When Jesus died on the Cross, most of those he called friends abandoned him, as witnessed by Peter's denial of Jesus. But the Gospels also model forgiveness and reconciliation between friends. Peter was reconciled to Jesus when the Risen Lord gave Peter a chance to redeem himself from his threefold denial by asking Peter three times to declare his love for the Lord. When Peter answered each time, "Yes, Lord, you know I love you," Jesus told him, "Feed my lambs . . . feed my sheep . . . follow me" (John 21:15–19). Peter was given the chance for spiritual friendship with Jesus again.

Also, at the foot of the Cross was a small band of family and friends: Mary, Jesus' Mother, Mary, the wife of Clopas, Mary Magdalene, and John, the "beloved disciple" (see John 19:25–27). This small group of faithful friends is sometimes called the "Little Company of Mary." Jesus invites all of us to this level of spiritual friendship with him. He says, "I no longer call you slaves, because a slave does not know what his master is doing. I have called you friends, because I have told you everything I have heard from my Father" (John 15:15). This is a profound statement for Jesus to make, since traditionally friendship is something that takes place between equals. It is comforting to know that God loved us so much that he was willing to make himself "equal" to us by becoming one of us through his Son, Jesus. It is indeed a radical thought, most profoundly proclaimed in Christianity, that human beings can have a deep and spiritual friendship with God.

Additionally, this type of close friendship, which we are called to with God, is also to be experienced through the friends we interact with in daily life. One of the most classic stories of spiritual friendship in the Bible is that of David and Jonathan. According to 1 Samuel 18:1, "Jonathan had become as fond of David as if his life depended on him; he loved him as he loved himself." Another example is the spiritual friendship of Ruth and Naomi: "Wherever you go I will go, and wherever you lodge I will lodge, your people shall be my people, and your God my God" (Ruth 1:16).

Additionally there are many examples of Christian saints for whom friendship was key to living a life of holiness. St. Gregory Nazianzen beautifully described the sense of spiritual friendship in a sermon in which he sang the praises of his friendship with St. Basil:

> Basil and I were both in Athens. We had come, like streams of a river, from the same source in our native land, had separated from each other in pursuit of learning, and were now united again as if by plan, for God so arranged it. . . . The same hope inspired us: the pursuit of learning. This is an ambition especially subject to envy. Yet between us there was no envy. On the contrary, we made capital out of our rivalry. Our rivalry consisted, not in seeking the first place for oneself but in yielding it to the other, for we each looked on the other's success as his own. We seemed to be two bodies with a single spirit.

Here are some other saints who shared deep spiritual friendships:

- Sts. Cyril and Methodius
- Sts. Benedict and Scholastica
- Sts. Francis and Clare
- Sts. John of the Cross and Teresa of Avila
- Sts. Perpetua and Felicity
- Sts. Cosmas and Damian
- Sts. Francis de Sales and Jane de Chantal

Also, many Christian martyrs are remembered along with their "companions, spiritual friends who were willing to lay down their lives to remain faithful to the true bond of their friendships: the love of God in Jesus Christ." The Church honors the following saints and their companions:

- St. Charles Lwanga and his companions, also known as the Ugandan Martyrs
- St. Isaac Jogues and his companions, also known as the North American Martyrs, the Canadian Martyrs, and the Martyrs of New France
- St. Paul Miki and his companions, also known as the Martyrs of Japan

All of these Christian saints recognized that the road that leads to holiness is best traveled with friends. Life itself is more meaningful when accompanied by friends. As Abraham Lincoln said, "The better part of one's life consists of his friendships."

It is important to emphasize that this notion of friendship is not just a nice idea to pursue. Friendship is at the very core of our nature. Scientists like to use the phrase "herd animals" when referring to human beings and our need for relationships. While that may be true, we humans have a deeper, spiritual need for relationships and friends than animals do. That need is due to our belief that we are made in the image and likeness of God—we are to "resemble" God.

FRIENDSHIPS ARE FACE-TO-FACE

While we are not equals with God, this concept of having a friendship with God conveys another very significant image, that of having a face-to-face encounter. While we can communicate with our friends in a variety of ways (texting, e-mailing, calling), nothing is better than an encounter in which we can see our friend's facial expressions, read their body language, and hear the tone of his or her voice. In a face-to-face friendship, we can have a true conversation.

I learned how important this is when I was a graduate student living in Rome for three-and-a-half years. This was the time before Internet, e-mail, and text messages, so communication with family and friends was usually limited to air-mail letters and expensive long-distance telephone calls. It was challenging to maintain strong relationships from afar. When I came home, it was essential to reestablish those face-to-face connections. I made sure to schedule focused one-on-one time with each of my family members and close friends soon after arriving back home.

Scripture tells us that Moses spoke to God "face to face, as one speaks to another" (Exodus 33:11). We, too, are invited to encounter God face-to-face, to enter into real conversation with him. St. Ignatius of Loyola made this a hallmark of his approach to prayer, teaching his followers that we pray well "by speaking to God as one friend speaks to another" (*The Spiritual Exercises*).

The very core of God's identity is a loving relationship of Three Persons—Father, Son, and Holy Spirit. The relationship between the Persons of the Trinity is so intimate that God is One. As beings created in the image of a Trinitarian God, we are called to live in a similar loving relationship with others. To do so is truly to reflect the image of God.

LOVE DEEPENS FRIENDSHIP

You may wonder how I, a Catholic bishop who took a priestly vow of celibacy, can speak of the necessity for intimate, loving relationships, the hallmark of friendship. Actually, the gift of celibacy is quite conducive to fostering intimate relationships. As a celibate priest and bishop, I am not called to refrain from relationships. On the contrary, my celibacy is a call to a radical relationship with God's people. Healthy celibacy is not maintained by avoiding relationships but rather by enabling me to enter into relationships with many people in profound ways at significant moments in their lives.

In my ministry I have often been amazed at how people whom I've never met before will open up to me and tell me some of their most intimate thoughts. Other priests describe the same experience. People have a deep sense that they can make a claim on a priest's availability, not only in the sense of time on his calendar, but in his emotional space where they feel the freedom and trust to pour out their joys and hopes, their griefs and their anxieties. The opening of the Second Vatican Council document *The Pastoral Constitution on the Church in the Modern World* echoes this same sentiment:

> The joys and the hopes, the griefs and the anxieties of the people of this age, especially those who are poor or in any way afflicted, these are the joys and hopes, the griefs and anxieties of the followers of Christ. Indeed, nothing genuinely human fails to raise an echo in their hearts.

I am blessed and privileged to have intimate and loving relationships with many different people, many different friends.

In our highly sexualized culture, people often confuse intimacy with sexual activity. Ironically, though, people can be physically close yet be miles apart from each other emotionally. Physical intimacy does not necessarily lead to emotional intimacy. That is why the Church has traditionally taught that sex is to be reserved for marriage, which is the total giving of oneself to the other, both emotionally and physically. But the emotional depth must be established before the physical expression of a relationship makes any real sense.

Celibacy, in contrast, allows for a depth of emotional intimacy with many people precisely because the commitment to a physical relationship has been excluded. In the business world, many companies have policies about personal relationships among employees, or at least between supervisors and their subordinates. Doctors have ethical prohibitions about sexual relationships with their patients, as well as lawyers with their clients. In all of these areas there is a strong sense that sexual expression will destroy other types of relationships that have a unique value all their own.

Love that is nonsexual is often called "platonic" because Plato described spiritual love between persons as preparatory for the love of God. St. Thomas Aquinas in his *Summa Theologiae* (questions 23–46 in section II–II) described the purest form of friendship as charity. For a true friendship to exist, there must be some common ground. While we will never be equal to God, we can imitate him. To increase our friendship with God, we must become more like him. We accomplish this by imitating God's charity in our relationships with others (see 1 John 4:8).

Finally, never forget that Jesus is a friend like no other! As the words of a great Christian hymn remind us, "What a friend we have in Jesus, all our sins and griefs to bear! What a privilege to carry everything to God in prayer!"

QUOTATION

Our soul is so specially loved by him who is the highest that it goes far beyond the ability of any creature to realize it. There is no creature made who can realize how much, how sweetly and how tenderly our maker loves us.

—Blessed Julian of Norwich

PROMISE

I will grow in my love for God by growing in the charity of spiritual friendship by . . .

PRAYER

O God, your Son Jesus calls us his friends, for he has made known to us everything that he heard from you. You give us strength and the promise of Salvation. Help us to be your faithful friends and caring companions for all those in need. Bring us to the glory of your heavenly kingdom, that we may share in the joy of seeing you face to face. We ask this through Christ our Lord. Amen.

STEP 8: FUN

Do we play to win? Do we play to have fun? Can we do both?

As I watched the 2012 London Olympic Games on television, I remembered how when my siblings and I were growing up, we couldn't resist turning the various rooms of our home into venues for our own version of the Olympics. Our poor mom. When I think of the damage we did to floors, walls, windows, and furniture—not to mention to one another—I can't help but think that she had the patience of a saint. In addition to the usual hockey, baseball, basketball, and football that took place in the Paprocki home, the Olympics inspired us to:

- jump hurdles over the furniture
- long jump in the living room

- shot put the paper weight
- sommersault in the kitchen
- spring the hallway
- spike the kitchen sponge

We also had a boxing and wrestling ring in one of our bedrooms. I know we had archery too. I'll have to ask one of my brothers for the details.

We did all of this, in our neverending quest to have fun, because fun is what kids do!

Fun was and continues to be a big part of Paprocki family life. Memories of my childhood are filled with laughter. In addition to playing sports, we enjoyed collecting and trading baseball cards, and playing board games such as Monopoly, Scrabble, Chinese checkers, Clue, Probe, and Mille Bornes (a French card game). We took photos of one another in silly costumes and poses. We created our own newspaper comic section. We tape-recorded ourselves telling jokes. To this day, when my family gets together, we tend toward silliness, taking a break from the *gravitas* of life and just taking pleasure in laughter and fun.

And sports have always been a key source of fun. As I mentioned earlier, I never thought of myself as an athlete as I was growing up. I simply saw sports as an outlet for having fun. In fact, some of the most fun that I have had over the years has been playing hockey when no one is keeping score.

Our seminary college campus had its own gym, athletic fields, baseball diamond, and tennis courts. I volunteered to serve on the athletic committee, and by my junior year I was running the entire intramural athletic program consisting of basketball, volleyball, touch football, tennis, ping-pong, weight lifting, and softball. I also served as sports information director, assisting the athletic director with the varsity sports program.

You may have noticed that I didn't mention hockey. When I got to college, hockey was not part of the program. When we were freshmen, we began to play anyway. We played floor hockey in the hallways and in a small workout gym in the lower level of the dormitory. We were having a blast, but a few broken windows and boisterous games that woke up faculty members in the middle of the night put an end to that. Fortunately, the athletic director, Coach Tom Kleeman, was a very wise and compassionate man who invited us to move our floor-hockey games into the main gym. A senior by the name of Bill Finn made nets out of wooden two-by-fours and chicken wire. We used those until Coach Kleeman felt sorry for us and bought us some real floor-hockey nets.

When I wasn't playing sports, I was officiating games. I spent most of my waking hours in the gym or the gym office. I kept up with my studies, but often read and wrote reports in the gym office too. My nickname in college was "Poppo." When people were looking for me, they'd ask, "Where's Poppo?" The answer was usually, "He's in the gym." I was a genuine gym rat. Sports played a big role in making college a blast!

Years later when I learned how to ice-skate and began playing ice hockey, I was thrilled to find out about something called "rat hockey." Having been a "gym rat," I immediately understood what it meant to be a "rink rat." Both expressions mean that you're such a regular part of the facility that you become part of the woodwork. More importantly, you get to play even if you're not that talented. I still enjoy going to the rink for a game of rat hockey, in which we just pick up sides and play, with no referees, no whistles, fewer rules, and most of all no scoreboard—except for the scoreboard in our heads, which we don't let detract us from having a great time.

THEY PLAY FOR FUN

Sports and athletics should be about nothing if not fun. Hall of Fame Dodger catcher Roy Campanella once explained that "you gotta be a man to play baseball for a living, but you have to have a lot of little boy in you, too." Back in Campy's time in baseball in the 1950s, professional teammates not only played together on the field; they usually played cards together when traveling, hung out for meals after the games, and even lived in the same neighborhood near the ballpark.

In fact, in the 1950s when professional-player salaries were more in line with those of other working people, the players blended into the neighborhood with the fans who came to watch them play. Dodgers Duke Snider, Carl Erskine, and Pee Wee Reese would often carpool to games. Duke Snider and his family joined in neighborhood block parties and would greet the children and teens of the neighborhood after games.

"A friend of mine used to walk Pee Wee Reese's daughter to school," said Florence Cozzolino, who lived in the Bay Ridge section of Brooklyn near some of the Dodgers. "They were so unpretentious. They really were. Baseball was different then. They weren't playing for the multimillions."

There are still plenty of professional athletes who play the game for fun. Consider Wes Timmons, a part-time PE teacher who played more than ten years in the minor leagues before getting a chance to be a reserve infielder with the Oakland A's in 2012. "As cliché as it sounds, it's really is for the love of the game. There's nothing I'd rather be doing than playing baseball," said Wes.

If you've ever shared the joy of hitting a ball on the nose, making a touchdown, scoring a goal (or preventing one!), finishing a race, smashing an overhead shot—the list goes on—then you know how fun sports can be. Even watching sports is supposed to be all about fun, no matter how often your team breaks your heart!

Newspaper reporters long ago dubbed the sports department of their newspapers as "the toy department." Most sports writers took the moniker—meant to be a bit mocking of the lack of importance in comparison of the two positions—as a compliment. Toy departments are fun! Sports are meant to be fun too!

FUN IS THE MOST IMPORTANT PART ABOUT SPORTS

Really, how many people join in a game of volleyball and a family picnic, sign up for a team, or compete in a 10K race in order to learn a life lesson of some kind? If we took a show of hands, would anyone admit to this?

Rather, sports and athletics *are* about having fun. Definitely the surveys on the subject reveal this to be true.

A famous study of youth sports done by a team at Michigan State University asked more than ten thousand junior high and high school students to list their twelve top reasons for participating in sports. At the top of the list for both boys and girls was "to have fun."

Girls listed "winning" as the least important reason; boys listed winning as eighth out of twelve.

This study also found out that the only way an athlete will continue to play sports—regardless of his or her athletic ability—is if they are having fun. Certainly reaching a high level of athletics demands hard work, sweat, and sacrifice. But if athletes find no fun in the practice, just all work and no play, they simply won't keep playing.

If you watched the gymnastics competition at the 2012 Olympics, you couldn't help but be enthralled by the joy that resonated from all-around gymnastics gold medalist, Gabby Douglas. Gabby certainly brought a level of serious proficiency to her competition, but it was hard for her to get through an entire routine without breaking out in a joyful smile. The fun that came from winning two gold Olympic medals (the other for the team competition) was the product of finding fun in the grueling workouts that preceded the Olympics.

"It means so much, all the hard work and dedication and effort put in the gym and hard days," Gabby explained. "And hard days are the best because that's where champions are made, so if you push through the hard days you can get through anything."

FUN IN GOD'S WORLD

How does God feel about having fun? Certainly, Christianity doesn't mean being dour and miserable. It's hard to believe this in our culture today when Christmas has become so commercialized, but there was a time when some Protestant Christians did not believe in celebrating Christmas at all. Bruce David Forbes, in his book *Christmas Was Not Always Like This: A Brief History*, writes that during the Reformation many Protestant churches saw Christmas as principally a Catholic holiday and played down its importance.

English Puritans and Scottish Presbyterians were especially vocal in their disapproval of the Christmas holiday. The loudest critics of Christmas were the English and American Puritans, but Calvinists and Presbyterians also took offense at the Catholic celebrations of the Christmas holiday. In 1644, the English Parliament passed a law saying that Christmas should be a day of penance rather than a feast day. By 1652, the observance of Christmas in England was forbidden throughout the realm, even in church. This ban carried over into the New World.

Catholicism countered this Protestant view by emphasizing the incarnational aspect of Christianity. What this means is that, because God became flesh and lived in this world, the world is meant to be celebrated and enjoyed. Fun is permitted! Don't forget when God created the world he viewed it as good (see Genesis 1:31).

This positive view of the Church toward fun does not mean that we should pursue pleasure with unbridled passion. The *Catechism of the Catholic Church* describes temperance as "the moral virtue that moderates the attraction of pleasures and provides balance in the use of created goods. It ensures the will's mastery over instincts and keeps desires within the limits of what is honorable" (1809). As the saying goes, all things in moderation.

Ultimately, God wants us to be happy, thus the very word "gospel" means "good news." In the Sermon on the Mount, Jesus gave us the Beatitudes, from the Latin word *beatus*, which means "happy" or "blessed." The ultimate joy is the beatific vision: seeing God face-to-face.

FUN AND LAUGHTER

Jokes, humor, and laughter are connected with having fun in sports and life. In his book *Between Heaven and Mirth: Why Joy, Humor, and Laughter Are at the Heart of the Spiritual Life*, Fr. Jim Martin, S.J., reminds us that humor contributes to healthy spirituality in at least three ways:

1. It is a tool for humility.
2. It speaks truth to power.

3. It reminds us that joy is an important part of our relationship with God.

In essence, Fr. Martin is telling us all to "lighten up." In his own words, here's why:

> For all its dignity and grandeur and gravity, the Christian church is, like any institution, manifestly human. With that humanity comes some laughter, both intentional and unintentional. This is a gift from God, who wants us to enjoy ourselves, to appreciate the absurdities of life, and not to take ourselves so seriously, particularly in religious institutions, where it's easy to become deadly serious.

He goes on to say,

> Joy, to begin with, is what we'll experience when we are welcomed into heaven. We may even laugh for joy when we meet God. Joy, a characteristic of those close to God, is a sign of not only a confidence in God, but also, as we will see in the Jewish and Christian Scriptures, gratitude for God's blessings. As the Jesuit priest Pierre Teilhard de Chardin said, "Joy is the most infallible sign of the presence of God."

In the joyful spirit of Fr. Martin's book, I offer one of my own favorite Catholic jokes. In the spirit of *this* book, it is a hockey joke, of course!

> A couple of nuns went to a hockey game. These nuns wore the traditional religious habit, and their large veils partially blocked the view of three men sitting behind the nuns. In an effort to get them to move, the first guy said in a very loud voice, "I think I'm going to move to Utah; there are only one hundred nuns living there." The second guy spoke up and said, "I want to go to Montana; there are only fifty nuns living there." The third guy said, "I want to go to Idaho; there are only twenty-five nuns living there." One of the nuns decided that she had heard enough, turned around, looked at the men, and in a very sweet, calm voice said, "Why don't you go to hell? There aren't any nuns there!"

As the saying goes, "Laughter is the best medicine!"

FUN AND THE CATHOLIC LIFE

What about being a Catholic and having fun? Isn't Catholic tradition all about penance, suffering, and denials of earthly desires? Actually, fun is a critical part of Catholic spirituality. In fact, *National Catholic Reporter* Vatican correspondent John Allen pointed out that the Catholic Church doesn't get enough credit for being a lot of fun:

> There's great warmth and laughter in most Catholic circles, a rich intellectual tradition, a vast body of lore, an incredible range of characters, a deep desire to do good, an abiding faith against all odds, an ability to go anywhere and feel instantly at home, and even a deep love of good food, good drink, and good company. All that is part of the tapestry of Catholic life, but it rarely sees the light of day in commentary and reporting that focuses exclusively on crisis, scandal, and heartache.

Likewise, in a 2008 *US Catholic* article, "It's Fun to Be Catholic," sociologist Fr. Andrew Greeley asserted:

> In its best moments Catholicism is the happiest of the major world religions. It is permeated by the reverent joy of Christmas night, the exultant joy of Easter morn, the gentle joy of First Communion, the satisfied joy of grammar school graduation, the hopeful joy of a funeral Mass, the confident joy of a May crowning. Catholicism is shaped by the happiness of hymns like "O Come, O Come,

> Emmanuel," "Adeste Fideles," the "Exultet," and "Bring Flowers of the Fairest."

Fr. Greeley went on to explain that Catholicism's focus on community is another dimension that lends itself to fun:

> It's more fun being Catholic because it's more fun to belong to something than to be a religious lone wolf. Catholics, as I say, tend to swarm. It is fun to belong to something, it is fun to believe that God is close to us, loving us like a spouse, a parent, a friend. That's why Catholics stick to their church, come what may. Despite the creeps and the party poopers, the puritans and the spoilsports, the killjoys and parade ruiners, Catholicism is too much fun to leave.

I couldn't agree more with these assessments. Believe me, in my work as a bishop, I encounter more than my fair share of challenging situations. However, in my daily encounters and travels, visiting parishes, schools, religious communities, hospitals, and various other Catholic institutions, I am blessed to deal with some of the happiest people on the face of the earth. Indeed, Catholics know how important it is to have fun, and they know how to have fun!

YOU CAN HAVE FUN

Finally, consider the story of another Olympian, Eric Liddell, a devout Christian who won the men's 400-meter running competition at the 1924 Olympics in Paris. In the Academy Award–winning film *Chariots of Fire*, Eric Liddell's character says, "I believe that God made me for a purpose, but he also made me fast. When I run, I feel his pleasure." Sports and all athletics are good fun. They can be even more fun when you think of God taking pleasure in your accomplishments. At times when I am running a marathon, I feel a rush of endorphins, reminding me that God is pleased when I use the talents and abilities that he gave me. How wonderful it is to be able to share in God's joy.

In seeking out fun in sports and athletics, continue to ask yourself these central questions:

- Do you play to win?
- Do you play to have fun?
- Can you do both?

I believe that you indeed can do both. Think again of the smile of Gabby Douglas, and also imagine all of the hours she toiled in the gym, when you have any doubts. Having fun, playing by the rules, and respecting your opponent doesn't relegate you to finishing last. You can still have fun even when the final score doesn't come out in your favor. What matters is that you will not be imprisoned by your fears, frustrations, and failures. With fortitude, faith, family, friendship, and fun, you can achieve your holy goals for body and soul.

May God give you this grace. Amen.

QUOTATION

We are not in our own power, but in the power of God.

—St. Perpetua

PROMISE

I will always keep the joy of sports central to my participation by remembering that . . .

PRAYER

O God, Creator of all that is good, you delight in the love of your children. May the fun that we seek always bring you honor. May our enjoyment of your creation always give you glory. May our achievements always bring you pleasure. Help us to be holy, that the holiness of our lives may lead to the happiness of sharing forever in the joy of your eternal love. We ask this through Christ our Lord. Amen.

Bishop Thomas John Paprocki is a native of Chicago's south side and presides over the Catholic Diocese of Springfield, Illinois. Bishop Paprocki has been playing hockey since the 1960s, often practicing in the basement of his father's pharmacy store with his six brothers; he currently plays goalie in a masters' hockey league. Bishop Paprocki has played goalie in practices with the Chicago Blackhawks and Columbus Blue Jackets of the National Hockey League. He also runs marathons; his current total is eighteen. Among his many Church appointments, Bishop Paprocki is the episcopal advisor for Catholic Athletes for Christ.

Joe Paprocki, younger brother of Bishop Thomas John Paprocki, has been active in pastoral ministry for over thirty years. The bestselling author of many resources for professional and volunteer catechists, including *The Catechist's Toolbox*, Joe Paprocki is currently a national consultant for faith formation at Loyola Press.

Founded in 1865, Ave Maria Press,
a ministry of the Congregation of
Holy Cross, is a Catholic publishing
company that serves the spiritual and
formative needs of the Church and its
schools, institutions, and ministers;
Christian individuals and families; and
others seeking spiritual nourishment.

For a complete listing of titles from

Ave Maria Press

Sorin Books

Forest of Peace

Christian Classics

visit www.avemariapress.com

AmP ave maria press® / Notre Dame, IN 46556
A Ministry of the United States Province of Holy Cross